RETHINKING THE KEYNESIAN REVOLUTION

RETHINKING THE KEYNESIAN REVOLUTION

Keynes, Hayek, and the Wicksell Connection

By Tyler Beck Goodspeed

OXFORD
UNIVERSITY PRESS

OXFORD
UNIVERSITY PRESS

Oxford University Press, Inc., publishes works that further
Oxford University's objective of excellence
in research, scholarship, and education.

Oxford New York
Auckland Cape Town Dar es Salaam Hong Kong Karachi
Kuala Lumpur Madrid Melbourne Mexico City Nairobi
New Delhi Shanghai Taipei Toronto

With offices in
Argentina Austria Brazil Chile Czech Republic France Greece
Guatemala Hungary Italy Japan Poland Portugal Singapore
South Korea Switzerland Thailand Turkey Ukraine Vietnam

Published by Oxford University Press, Inc.
198 Madison Avenue, New York, New York 10016
www.oup.com

Library of Congress Cataloging-in-Publication Data
Goodspeed, Tyler Beck.
Rethinking the Keynesian revolution : Keynes, Hayek, and the
Wicksell connection / by Tyler Beck Goodspeed.
p. cm.
Includes bibliographical references and index.
ISBN 978-0-19-984665-8 (cloth :alk. paper) 1. Keynesian economics.
2. Keynes, John Maynard, 1883–1946. 3. Hayek,
Friedrich A. von (Friedrich August), 1899–1992. 4. Wicksell, Knut, 1851–1926.
I. Title.
HB99.7.G656 2012
330.15′6—dc23
2011051633

3 5 7 9 8 6 4 2
Printed in the United States of America
on acid-free paper

For Professor Medoff

CONTENTS

RETHINKING THE KEYNESIAN REVOLUTION

INTRODUCTION: RETHINKING THE KEYNESIAN REVOLUTION

Reflecting on a Keynesian revolution of which he himself was a principal architect, Nobel laureate Sir John Hicks remarked that "when the definitive history of economic analysis during the 1930s comes to be written, a leading character in the drama (it was quite a drama) will be Professor Hayek." Though Friedrich von Hayek's economic writings "are almost unknown to the modern student," Hicks observed, "there was a time when the new theories of Hayek were the *principal* rival of the new theories of Keynes. Which was right, Keynes or Hayek?"[1]

After a hiatus of a few decades, Hicks's question is once again in vogue among macroeconomists. The academic consensus that coalesced, in the decade preceding 2008, around a standard "dynamic stochastic general equilibrium" class of economic model has since frayed. Indeed, IMF chief economist Olivier Blanchard's August 2008 declaration that "the state of macro is good," and that "a largely shared vision both of fluctuations and of methodology has emerged"—a sentiment echoed as late as January 2009 in the macroeconomic issue of the *American Economic Journal*, by Michael Woodford's rather ironically (in retrospect) titled article "Convergence in Macroeconomics: Elements of the New Synthesis"—seems subsequently to have given way to a sense of crisis, and awkward discord, in the economics profession not seen since Milton Friedman declared the death of the Phillips curve in 1968, or possibly even since Keynes and Hayek sparred in the pages of the *Economic Journal* in 1932. Both men have thus been duly hauled out of, at times, ignominious retirement as standard-bearers of competing visions of the operation of a market economy. A comedic "Keynes vs. Hayek" YouTube rap, along with an encore sequel, even went viral in 2010–2011.

From the perspective of the history of economics, however, "Keynes or Hayek" is in many respects a flawed question; the consensus that ultimately emerged, and, discord notwithstanding, largely persists still in modern macroeconomics is neither "Keynesian" nor "Hayekian" but rather unmistakably "Walrasian." Moreover, contrary to the popularized rivalry, Keynes and Hayek not only shared far more theoretical ground than is typically realized but also held a deeper theoretical affinity with one another than with modern macro.

The source of that affinity, I argue, is the "Wicksell connection." It effectively ended with Keynes and Hayek. As the following family tree of twentieth-century macroeconomics illustrates, since the merger of the quantity theory tradition of Irving Fisher with Walrasian general equilibrium, by Robert Lucas and the "New Classicals," all mainstream schools of macroeconomic thought, including both the real business cycle theorists and the so-called New Keynesians, have adhered to the Walrasian approach.[2] Of the postwar Keynesian schools, only flotsam and jetsam remain. We are all Walrasians now.

The notion of a Wicksell connection was first conceived by economist Axel Leijonhufvud in the mid-1970s, a time of acute crisis for the New Keynesians' "Neoclassical Keynesian" predecessors, to

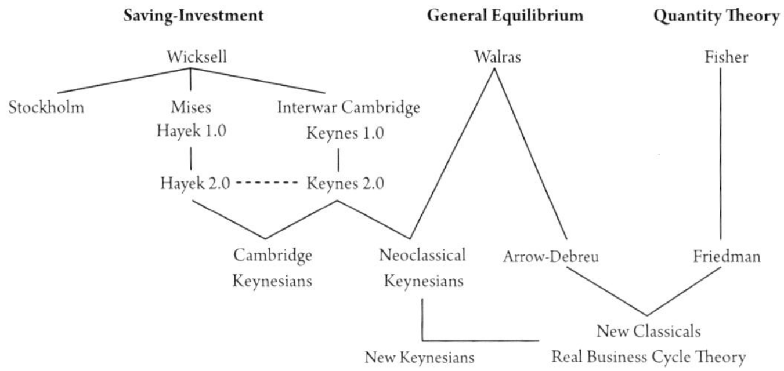

Figure I.1

highlight Keynes's kinship with a theoretical approach to monetary economics, separate from the quantity theory line of Irving Fisher and Milton Friedman, established by late nineteenth-century Swedish economist Knut Wicksell. Unlike the quantity theory and Walrasian traditions, which assume the rate of interest either to always and perfectly coordinate saving and investment or else to reduce it, in the latter case, to merely an infinite set of simultaneously determined intertemporal price ratios, the Wicksellian approach hoists the problem of intertemporal coordination front and center, with the interest rate as the decisive variable.

It is the argument of this book that not only did Keynes and Hayek *both* adhere to the Wicksellian approach, but also that the Wicksell "connection" was, as a result, responsible for a fundamental *convergence* of their respective theories of money, capital, and the business cycle during the course of the 1930s. In short, Keynes and Hayek were not quite the theoretical antagonists they were, and have since been, made out to be.

Our Wicksell "connection" linking, or bridging the gap between, Keynes and Hayek consists of three primary themes, all of them tightly interrelated. The first is that money matters. From the perspective of economic theory, this is a by no means trivial point. Joseph Schumpeter described it as the difference between *real* and *monetary* analysis. The former assumes that monetary issues may be analyzed separately from the determination of equilibrium in a system of perfect barter, introduced at a later stage without disrupting the results of preceding stages of analysis in strictly real terms, while the latter maintains that money must be admitted into our analysis from, so to speak, "the ground floor."[3] Assessing neo-Walrasian models of general equilibrium, Frank Hahn rather bleakly concludes that not only is money an "inessential property" of any general equilibrium model, but also that "there is nothing we can say about the equilibrium of an economy with 'money' that one cannot say about the equilibrium of a non-monetary economy."[4] As Hahn points out, all approaches of Walrasian descent accordingly reside squarely and immovably in the real analysis camp; money is and can only be an "inessential property."[5]

The core of the Wicksell connection is, in contrast, the integration of real with monetary analysis. As Hayek noted in his *Prices and Production* (1931), "The task of monetary theory is . . . nothing less than to cover a second time the whole field which is treated by pure theory under the assumption of barter, and to investigate what changes in the conclusions of pure theory are made necessary by the introduction of indirect exchange."[6] For there exists, he argued, a "fundamental diversity" between a monetary economy, and the pure barter economy assumed in general equilibrium.[7] Even in his *Pure Theory of Capital* (1941)—the "pure" referring to the explicitly and strictly real terms of analysis—Hayek was keen to note that the work was intended to be merely preparatory to the larger task of integrating money into a dynamic theory of capital accumulation. Keynes, outlining his vision of the still inchoate *General Theory*, similarly announced his migration from real toward monetary analysis. His own theory, he wrote, "In contradistinction to" the theory of a "real-exchange economy" in which money exists but serves "merely as a neutral link between transactions in real things and real assets," would deal rather "with an economy in which money plays a part of its own and affects motives and decisions and is, in short, one of the operative factors in the situation, so that the course of events cannot be predicted either in the long period or in the short, without a knowledge of the behavior of money between the first state and the last." This, he declared is what "we ought to mean when we speak of *a monetary economy*."[8] The neo-Walrasian theorist hence acquits himself of the very task to which both Keynes and Hayek assigned economic theory.

The neutrality of money is, in fact, a pillar of modern monetary theory; even the New Keynesians have evacuated any defense of monetary non-neutrality beyond the very short run. The classical dichotomy of layering an absolute price level atop an otherwise perfectly operating system of pure barter remains in high regard. The question we must ask, however, is whether it is in fact valid to suppose that an economy which in reality could not function without money, will be unaffected by its addition to our analysis? In other words, does it make sense to claim that the equilibrium established in a hypothetical barter economy will be the same as that in a monetary economy, despite the fact that the former could never obtain in the absence of money?[9] As a monetary theorist, Wicksell was saliently concerned precisely with "what occurs, in the first place, with the middle link in the final exchange of one good against another, which is formed by the demand of money for goods and the supply of goods against money."[10] This seemingly self-evident insight, however, would prompt what Bertil Ohlin called Wicksell's "most fruitful innovation." That is, recognizing that a rise in the general price level owes to a rise in total demand relative to supply, and that the interest rate is charged with the dual task of both regulating excess demand for money and intermediating between the separate decisions to save and invest, Wicksell realized that it would be worthwhile to divide supply and demand into two categories—the supply of consumer goods and the supply of capital goods, in the first instance, and income intended to be spent and income intended to be saved, in the second.[11]

In Wicksell's system, then, fluctuations in output stem from the failure of the rate of interest to successfully coordinate saving and investment at all times. By superimposing the market for credit on to the market for real capital, and then inserting financial intermediation between the separate decisions to save and invest, Wicksell in effect distended the link between what he termed the "natural" rate of interest and the "money," or "bank," rate of interest. It was then the potential divergence of these two rates, between a hypothetical real rate of return on physical capital and the prevailing market price of credit, that could disrupt the equality of saving and investment, and thereby initiate a cumulative movement away from an initial position of equilibrium. Money, therefore, far from functioning merely as an inessential numéraire or transaction constraint, as in the Fisherian and Walrasian schemas, instead constitutes a kind of "loose joint," to borrow Hayek's term, in the operation of the intertemporal price mechanism.[12] But—and this is the crucial difference between Wicksellian Keynesianism and later Neoclassical and New Keynesianism—the transmission of a monetary shock is first and foremost through its effect on the (*ex ante*) gap between saving and investment, *not*, as both monetarists and "Keynesians," old and young, would have it, through its derivative effect on unanticipated inflation.

Money, therefore, is intimately related to the second element of the Wicksell connection, namely, the identification of intertemporal coordination as the central problem in macroeconomics. As Keynes was keen to point out, "The importance of money essentially flows from its being a link between the present and the future."[13] Similarly, Hayek would note that "so long as we assume entrepreneurs to decide every detail in advance in the certain expectation that they will be able to adhere to all their plans, the need for holding money almost vanishes. For in the actual world money is largely held because the decision as to when to buy or to pay for something is deliberately postponed."[14] Consequently, unless we assume by the very formulation of our model that the conditions of monetary equilibrium rule out from the start the existence of a rate of interest that would render saving and investment plans inconsistent, and thus in a state of disequilibrium, then we must ask by what mechanism disparate expectations and plans for the future are to be reconciled. If, in other words, we *define* the relationship between output and the rate of interest as a *first-order condition* of intertemporal equilibrium, then we are effectively disallowing the very misalignment between the money rate of interest and the rate that would render consumption and investment plans compatible.[15]

Critical to the Wicksellian approach, therefore, is the notion that producers, consumers, and investors need not be acting on the basis of mutually *consistent* expectations. Rather, the Wicksellian economy is one that gives full scope to potential coordination failure, with the "dark forces of time and ignorance," poised always to disrupt the coincidence of saving and investment.[16] While such coordination failures are exceedingly difficult to generate in atemporal or metastatic Walrasian models, they lie at the very core of Wicksell-Keynes-Hayek research agenda, of both pre- and post-1936 vintages. For implicit in Wicksell's analytical division of supply and demand into consumer and capital goods, and income saved and spent, is an indictment of the quantity theory's divorce of discussions of the general price level from the Neoclassical theory of pricing and distribution, or, more precisely, between monetary and price theory. It is, he perceived, predominantly changes in *relative* prices, and specifically the relative prices of consumer and capital goods, that are characteristic of price movements.[17]

This is by no means a purely academic point. The bottom line of the Wicksell-Keynes-Hayek story is that if saving exceeds investment, then relative prices are "wrong," which means that no amount of flexibility on the part of the general price level (nor, for that matter, on the part of nominal wages), will resolve what is in effect a failure of intertemporal coordination. If there is an "incorrect" price rigidity—incorrect in the sense of being inconsistent with full employment—to be indicted, then it is to be found in the market for financial assets, not in the markets for goods or labor.[18] In other words, if the real interest rate fails to coordinate saving and investment plans, we cannot then simply rely upon flexible wages and goods prices to do the job in its stead. A problem that requires, as a solution, an interest rate at a level that raises the relative current demand price of capital goods will not be resolved by the Pigou effect.

Which leads us, then, to the third and final theme constituting our Wicksell connection. The problem of intertemporal coordination of economic activity, the defeat of "the dark forces of time and ignorance," as Keynes put it, is inextricably bound up with questions concerning the dispersion, acquisition, and distribution of information and knowledge. Whether and how a market system can coordinate the contingent plans of manifold individuals with discrete and often inconsistent knowledge is therefore perhaps the most fundamental component of the Wicksell connection. Both Keynes and Hayek, as it were, struggled to escape the invisible hand of the Walrasian auctioneer, with Keynes demonstrating how the coordination of individual economic activity could break down, while Hayek explored the conditions under which the market could ever get it right. Their theoretical analyses were thus not so much opposed to one another as they were just nonoverlapping in focus.

In either case, it is tempting to conclude that Keynes and Hayek were fundamentally focused on the economics of rigidities—price "stickiness," in conventional parlance. The mistaken equation of

Keynesian economics with the assumption of sticky prices is sufficiently well known that it need not detain us here.[19] But Hayek, too, took umbrage with the characterization of his theory as being, ultimately, a story of price "lags." Responding to Hicks's suggestion that what he was really talking about was a lag in money prices behind changes in the real data—nominal rigidities, in other words—Hayek declared that the notion of some definite "lag" was based on the "unfounded and erroneous" conception of equilibrium as "a structure of relative prices determined only by the *real* factors" that will "restore itself promptly after being disturbed by the first impact of a monetary change, even while the change itself... still continues."[20] Hayek acknowledged that, by this reasoning, his own theory might be described as one of "disequilibrium,"—he preferred an analogy to "fluid equilibrium"—but the bottom line was that the fundamental issue was not price lags, per se, but rather the process of continuous adjustment to changes in economic data.

To put the same point in general equilibrium terms, we might say that, for Keynes and Hayek, as for Wicksell, the generation of economic fluctuations requires not that prices be "rigid," nor even that they, as a rule, adjust at slower velocities than output, but simply that their inability to adjust instantaneously and with perfect coordination allows for trading to occur at "false," or non-market-clearing, prices. Inasmuch as agents, in response to a change in economic data, are unable to *immediately* and *simultaneously* effect the traverse from one vector of market-clearing prices to another, then we must admit the possibility of trades occurring at false prices, in which case the equilibrium which *would* have obtained, in the presence of "perfect" price flexibility, becomes informative only insofar as it provides an analytical stepping stone for the study of *dynamics*. Here, the first of our Wicksellian themes has an important role to play. In the absence of the Walrasian auctioneer, or his rational agent equivalent, it is the job of the monetary system to convey information—about costs, endowments, production possibilities, tastes, demand—through prices. The danger is that while money might provide a liquidity buffer against the destabilizing consequences of trades taking place at non-market-clearing prices, it also permits such trades to take place in the first place.[21] The challenge, in the Wicksell-Keynes-Hayek program, is thus to explain how the economy will behave *outside* of Walrasian equilibrium, to describe the dynamic processes by which the economy might gravitate toward equilibrium and, if so, toward which?

Many of the points presented in this book will not strike the historian of economics as wholly new. First and foremost, the historian of economic thought will detect strong echoes of arguments Axel Leijonhufvud has been making since at least 1968, particularly as concerns issues relating to economics as an information and coordination problem.[22] David Laidler has written extensively on, to again borrow Hayek's words, the "fundamental diversity" between a monetary economy and the real economy of Walrasian general equilibrium.[23] Ludwig Lachmann elaborated the theoretical insights of Hayek's *Pure Theory of Capital* far more thoroughly than I could hope to do here, and my discussions of capital, time, and equilibrium trespass upon ground for which I owe Geoff Harcourt and Avi Cohen thanks for having previously plowed.[24] But the purpose of this book is not to assert new theory, nor even to claim (re)discovery of old. Rather, it is to bring together in one narrative multiple disparate strands that I believe unite, or at the very least reconcile, the research agendas of two supposedly polarly opposed economic thinkers and, in so doing, suggest a reorientation of current economic research. Indeed, to those who might ask whether we ought to go back to Keynes or rather Hayek in order to move forward in economics, my answer is yes.

The following chapters are thus structured so as to trace the Wicksellian theme(s) through its various Keynesian and Hayekian iterations. Chapter 1 introduces and defines the Wicksell connection as it appeared in Wicksell's own economic writings, drawing attention in particular to the close interdependence of the real and monetary dimensions of Wicksell's "cumulative process." The essential point is to demonstrate that it is only through the introduction of the Böhm-Bawerkian element of time, or "roundaboutness," into the capitalistic structure of production that Wicksell is able to sustain the conclusions of his model. In so doing, however, he exposes his natural-rate mechanism to considerable complications in the theory of capital, namely, the circular dependence of the value of capital on the rate of interest. Chapter 2 constructs a parallel analysis of the first Keynesian and Hayekian variations of Wicksell's two-rates framework (Keynes and Hayek 1.0, in our family tree), concluding with an analytical interpolation between the two theories to identify the points of both commonality and theoretical cleavage. The third section of this chapter emphasizes especially the manner in which both economists incorporate relative prices into Wicksell's cumulative process to derive theories of cyclical fluctuations around otherwise stable equilibria.

Chapter 3 confronts what we will call the "Sraffa connection," focusing on the pivotal role played by Keynes's fellow Cantabrigian Piero Sraffa in fully exposing the capital-theoretic vulnerabilities of the Wicksellian approach that lingered in Keynes and Hayek 1.0, and, specifically, the meaninglessness of the concept of *a* natural rate of interest in a multicommodity world. The Sraffa connection, I will argue, in fact comprises the analytical linchpin to the entire reconciliation of the Wicksell connection between Keynes and Hayek; his terse, twelve-page review of Hayek's *Prices and Production* ultimately, if unintentionally, provided the essential building block, in the form of "commodity rates of interest," of the Wicksell-esque theories of capital and interest presented in both Keynes's *General Theory* and Hayek's 1941 *Pure Theory of Capital*.

Chapters 4 and 5 thus analyze these final two iterations of the Wicksell connection (Keynes and Hayek 2.0 in our tree), demonstrating that Keynes's and Hayek's reconstitutions of Wicksell's natural rate in terms of the rate of return on investment (Keynes's "marginal efficiency of capital," Hayek's "marginal value product of investment") represent the culmination of the Wicksellian natural-money rate schema, capital-theoretic complications and all. Taken together, despite the considerable attention paid to the issues raised in the Cambridge Capital Controversies concerning the problems of "Wicksell effects," chapters 4 and 5 demonstrate that as far as Keynes and Hayek are concerned, the capital controversies are something of a sideshow and, particularly in Hayek's case, a red herring, in the sense that both economists ultimately managed to avoid getting bogged down in the intractable issues of measuring and valuing capital that consumed previous (and subsequent) Neoclassical theorists, without having to resort to the timeless, metastatic approach of neo-Walrasian general equilibrium.[25]

The book thus concludes, in chapter 6, by situating the Keynes-Hayek debates within the broader context of the history of economic thought, looking both backward to Wicksell and forward to the more substantive, and less esoteric and acrimonious, issues of the Cambridge Capital Controversies—questions of time, capital, and equilibrium—and to the modern neo-Walrasian hegemony, specifically the ubiquitous "New Keynesian," or "New Neoclassical Synthesis" dynamic stochastic general equilibrium (DSGE) models. In this chapter, I furthermore explore the policy dimension of Keynes's and Hayek's accord, revealing that, unsurprisingly given the theoretical affinities, neither was Keynes as cavalier with respect to inflation, nor Hayek as austere with respect to deep depression, as partisans on both sides have tended to suggest.

To be clear, the aim here is not to rehash old debates; there is a conspicuous whiff of necrophilia where one exhumes old theories and resurrects old theoreticians for deployment in contemporary intellectual battles. Nor, however, is the aim to impose theoretical, let alone policy, accord where none existed; Keynes and Hayek, to be sure, had much to disagree on in the realm of economic theory.[26] Rather, my objective is to clarify the (imperfect) role of the real interest rate in coordinating intertemporal economic activity, and to situate that mechanism within larger questions about money, equilibrium, and dynamics, by retracing the development of a theoretical approach which identified these issues as together comprising the core of the economic problem. Keynes and Hayek, following Wicksell's lead, both viewed the adjustment *process* of real variables in a monetary economy, and the pivotal role played by the rate of interest in that process, as the essential challenge in macroeconomic theory. For both, while monetary variables may represent the conduit of crisis, real variables constitute it, and on this point the Wicksellian money-natural rate legacy is crucial, giving full scope not only to money as an essential property of a capital-using economy but also to the entire host of issues and complications relating to uncertainty and expectations that the introduction of money entails. Ultimately, this fundamental common ground united the two economists more than perhaps even they, in Kuhnian sleepwalking fashion, managed to apprehend.

Critically, then, surveying the genealogical typology of *The General Theory* in this manner does not assume a priori that Keynes was necessarily "revolutionary." Revolution implies a degree of discontinuous change; the very fact that we can identify and trace a common Wicksellian "theme" through its various Keynesian and Hayekian guises would seem to defy such a label. Moreover, if there was a Keynesian revolution, whatever it was, it was almost certainly fought under a Wicksellian banner, and in that respect Hayek, far from being a rival, was a compatriot.

NOTES

1. John R. Hicks, "The Hayek Story," in *Critical Essays in Monetary Theory* (Oxford: Clarendon Press, 1967), 203.
2. This diagram is adapted from a similar figure employed by Axel Leijonhufvud in his 1981 paper. I have expanded the tree to incorporate the Walrasian line, which has come to dominate mainstream macroeconomics since the 1970s as a distinct tradition. I have also indicated the Walrasian character of the "Neoclassical Keynesians," or the Keynesians of the "Neoclassical Synthesis." See Axel Leijonhufvud, "The Wicksell Connection: Variations on a Theme," in *Information and Coordination: Essays in Macroeconomic Theory* (New York: Oxford University Press, 1981), 131.
3. Joseph Schumpeter, *History of Economic Analysis* (1954; reprint, London: Routledge, 2006), 264–265.
4. F.H. Hahn, "On the Foundations of Monetary Theory," in *Essays in Modern Economics*, M. Parkin, ed. (London: Longman, 1973), 231.
5. See Colin Rogers, *Money, Interest and Capital: A Study in the Foundations of Monetary Theory* (Cambridge: Cambridge University Press, 1989), 3–4 for a more thorough summary of Real vs. Monetary Analysis. It should, however, be noted that Rogers places Wicksell within the "real analysis" camp. Though it is true that long-run equilibrium in Wicksell's model is established by real forces, we contend here that by focusing on the process of adjustment to a new equilibrium, and the monetary forces involved in that process, Wicksell's analysis is pointing in the direction of closer affinity with monetary versus pure real analysis.
6. F. A. Hayek, *Prices and Production* (London: Routledge, 1931; reprint, New York: Augustus M. Kelley, 1967), 127.
7. Ibid., 44.
8. J.M. Keynes, "A Monetary Theory of Production," (1933), reprinted in *The Collected Writings of John Maynard Keynes*, vol. 13, "The General Theory and After: Part I Preparation" (London and Basingstoke: Macmillan, 1973), 408–409.
9. F.A. Hayek, *The Pure Theory of Capital* (Chicago: University of Chicago Press, 1941), 31.
10. Knut Wicksell, *Lectures on Political Economy*, vol. 2, Money, ed. Lional Robins, trans. E. Classen (1906; reprint, London: Routledge & Kegan Paul, 1935), 159. Emphasis in original. The Wicksell-Hayek link on this point is also made by Gerald O'Driscoll, in Gerald P. O'Driscoll, *Economics as a Coordination Problem: The Contributions of Friedrich A. Hayek* (Kansas City, MO: Sheed Andrews and McMeel, 1977), 40.
11. Bertil Ohlin, introduction to Knut Wicksell, *Interest and Prices: A Study of the Causes Regulating the Value of Money*, trans. R. F. Kahn (1898; reprint, London: Macmillan, 1936), xiv.

12. The analogy of a "loose joint" comes Hayek, *Pure Theory*, 408.
13. Keynes, *General Theory*, 293.
14. Hayek, *Pure Theory*, 29.
15. Mauro Boianovsky and Hans-Michael Trautwein, "The New Neoclassical Synthesis and the Wicksell-Keynes Connection," in *The Return to Keynes*, ed. Bradley W. Bateman, Toshiaki Hirai, Maria Cristina Marcuzzo (Cambridge, MA: Harvard University Press, 2010), 124.
16. J. M. Keynes, *The General Theory of Employment, Interest and Money* (1936; reprint, Cambridge: Cambridge University Press, 1973), 155.
17. Ohlin, introduction to Wicksell, *Interest and Prices*, xiv.
18. Boianovsky and Trautwein, "The New Neoclassical Synthesis," 124.
19. See, for instance, Paul Davidson, *John Maynard Keynes* (London: Palgrave Macmillan, 2009); Axel Leijonhufvud, *On Keynesian Economics and the Economics of Keynes: A Study in Monetary Theory* (London: Oxford University Press, 1968); Stephen Marglin, "Keynes without Nominal Rigidities," Harvard Institute of Economic Research Discussion Paper Number 1907 (2000).
20. F.A. Hayek, "3 Elucidations of the Ricardo Effect," *The Journal of Political Economy* 77 (1969), 278–279. Hayek was responding, specifically, to Hicks, "The Hayek Story," 206.
21. For an excellent discussion of these issues, see David Laidler, "The Monetary Economy and the Economic Crisis," Duke University Center for the History of Political Economy Working Paper No. 2011–04 (January 2011).
22. Especially Leijonhufvud, *On Keynesian Economics* and Leijonhufvud, "The Wicksell Connection." See also Leijonhufvud, *Information and Coordination*.
23. Laidler, "The Monetary Economy."
24. Ludwig Lachmann, *Capital and Its Structure* (Kansas City, MO: Sheed Andrews and McMeel, 1956); Avi Cohen and Geoff Harcourt, "Introduction: Capital Theory Controversy: Scarcity, Production, Equilibrium and Time," in *Capital Theory*, ed. Christopher Bliss, Avi J. Cohen, and G. C. Harcourt, vol. 1 (Cheltenham: Edward Elgar, 2005), xxvii–lx.
25. I thank Avi Cohen for pointing this out.
26. See, for example, G. R. Steele, *Keynes and Hayek: The Money Economy* (London: Routledge, 2001).

Chapter 1

The Wicksell Connection

According to Leijonhufvud, the interest rate mechanism "is the center of the confusion in modern macroeconomics."[1] Whether and how the interest rate manages to coordinate *both* the supply and demand for money *and* saving and investment jointly is the essence of what he calls the "Wicksell connection," Keynes's "obfuscation" of which effectively threw the baby of intertemporal coordination out with the bathwater of a loanable funds theory of interest.[2] Only by retracing the Wicksell connection through its various iterations, culminating in Keynes's 1936 "cover-up" and Hayek's oft-ignored *Pure Theory of Capital*, can we hope to reconcile the two along the lines of their common theoretical heritage.

Precisely what constitutes the Wicksellian theme, however, is by no means clear-cut. The great synthesizer of Neoclassical economics was known for his work not only in monetary theory and business cycle fluctuations but also in capital theory, value, and distribution. As George Shackle put it in his preface to the English language translation of Wicksell's *Value, Capital, and Rent* (1893), "Wicksell's work was like a mountain from whose flanks divergent streams run down and bring fertility to widely separated fields, only to merge again later into a single broad river."[3] Leijonhufvud singled out the maladjustment of the money and natural rates of interest within a loanable funds framework, while Don Patinkin emphasized Wicksell's "cumulative process" as an account of transitory disturbances around an equilibrium growth path.[4] In her 1956 effort to apply Keynes's short-run theory of income determination to the problem of long-run growth, *The Accumulation of Capital*, Joan Robinson declared Wicksell's theory of capital valuation to be "the key to the whole theory of accumulation and of the determination of wages and profits."[5] Some "connection."

As we will see later, the Wicksell connection, at least for the purposes of this study, is in fact twofold, straddling both monetary and capital theory. The signature feature of Wicksell's model is a persistent differential between a "money" and "natural" rate of interest, strictly correlated with the deviation of investment from planned saving. That this deviation can arise, however, results from Wicksell's recognition that in the circular flow of income through households, banks, and firms, there is no guarantee that all transactors will be operating under a mutually consistent set of information and expectations. In Wicksell's eyes, it is thus entirely conceivable that the nonbanking sector can in fact be misled by realized market prices, namely, the price of money.[6] Insofar as banks and firms consequently act on the basis of incorrect or imperfect information, the money rate of interest will be "wrong," which means that real saving will exceed or fall short of real investment, according as the money rate is too high or low.

The question is what, then, to make of the extensive theory of capital for which Wicksell was to later be the subject of intense academic debate. How does a theory that relates the valuation of capital to changes in the real wage and rate of interest impinge in any way upon a story of monetary maladjustment? In fact, however, Wicksell's monetary theory cannot be divorced from his theory of capital, and attempts to do so risk undermining the very foundations upon which the former was predicated. It is only through his theory of capital as a time-consuming process of production that Wicksell is able to merge the nominal and real dimensions of his model; without it, the Wicksellian "cumulative" process simply would not be cumulative. To speak of a Wicksell "connection" in the history of the Keynesian revolution thus requires confronting both the interest maladjustment within the loanable funds framework and the capital-theoretic foundations that permitted Wicksell to detach the real and money rates of interest.

1.1. WICKSELL'S MONETARY THEORY

Our account begins with Wicksell's so-called cumulative process. For Wicksell, the challenge facing monetary theory was to explain how the economy traverses from one quantity-theoretic equilibrium to another; that is, to describe the process of price adjustment to a change in the supply of money. The static propositions of the quantity theory, he argued, were insufficient for analyzing the movement of money and prices from one level to another, and for identifying the initiator of that movement. More specifically, he asked, how does one reconcile the quantity theory with "Gibson's Paradox," namely, the observed positive correlation between the rate of interest and general price level—the exact opposite of what we would expect in a purely quantity-theoretic world.[7]

The crux of the Wicksell connection thus consists of Wicksell's fundamental distinction between a real, or "natural," rate of interest on capital and the rate of interest actually prevailing in the market for credit, or the "money" rate of interest.[8] The former, Wicksell elaborates, corresponds to the interest rate that would obtain if, in the absence of credit, borrowing and lending were transacted only in the form of real capital goods, while the latter refers to the intermediary role of the banking system in the coordination of household savings and capital investment. The distinction implies not only that banks might lend less than the inward flow of savings from the household sector but also that they might extend as credit an amount greater than that inward flow. In other words, investment may vary independently of saving by the net addition to the supply of loanable funds provisioned by banks. The money rate of interest, as it were, unfetters investment from the strictures of Say's law.

At any moment, then, it is the natural rate which constitutes the rate of interest that will secure both the equality of saving and investment and, as a corollary, price-level stability. This must be the case, Wicksell argues, because if the supply of real savings exceeds or falls short of the expected real return on capital, then the consequent excess demand for investment must necessarily give rise to price inflation, and mutatis mutandis in the case of excess savings supply. Thus, if money "is loaned at this same rate of interest, it serves as nothing more than a cloak to cover a procedure which, from the purely formal point of view, could have been carried on equally well without it."[9] The rate of interest on money, however, "is a matter for negotiation with the owners of money and not with the owners of goods," meaning there is no reason to assume that the money rate will be equal to the natural rate; in fact, it almost never will.

The problem, in Wicksell's view, is that bankers and entrepreneurs need not be operating under the same set of information and expectations. The money rate of interest is, to a large extent, a product of "custom and tradition, in a word—routine."[10] That is, "As regards bank-rate policy, there is a far stronger reason for the maintenance of fixed rules of conduct. For neither an individual bank nor the banks of an individual country can on their own initiative embark on any change without keeping in accord with the procedure adopted by other banks."[11] As a result, the money rate of interest will be characterized by a certain degree of inertia. But the natural rate, in contrast, depends itself "on all the thousand and one things which determine the current economic position of a community; and with them it constantly fluctuates."[12] We have thus an incipient dilemma—the equality of saving and investment, and price-level stability, are secured solely by means of the equality of the money and natural rates of interest. But whereas the latter is neither fixed nor invariable, the former is to a certain extent petrified by custom, meaning every shift, however small, in the natural rate will likely give rise to disequilibrium in the market for loanable funds, and inflation (or deflation).

Consider, for instance, the case of an upward shift in the investment demand schedule, from I_0 to I_1, corresponding to a rise in the natural rate of interest from r_0 to r_1, as shown in figure 1.1.1. At the *old* rate of interest, there exists now an excess demand for commodities in the amount of $I_1(r_0) - S(r_0)$. In the absence of any countervailing action on the part of banks, the money rate will track the natural rate pari passu, rising also from r_0 to r_1. Consumption demand falls by $S(r_1) - S(r_0)$, and for capital goods by $I_1(r_0) - I_1(r_1)$, such that any incipient excess demand is eliminated. The economy transitions to a new, higher growth path. If, however, banks, on account of "custom and tradition," hold the natural rate at r_0, $I_1(r_0) - S(r_0)$ will correspond

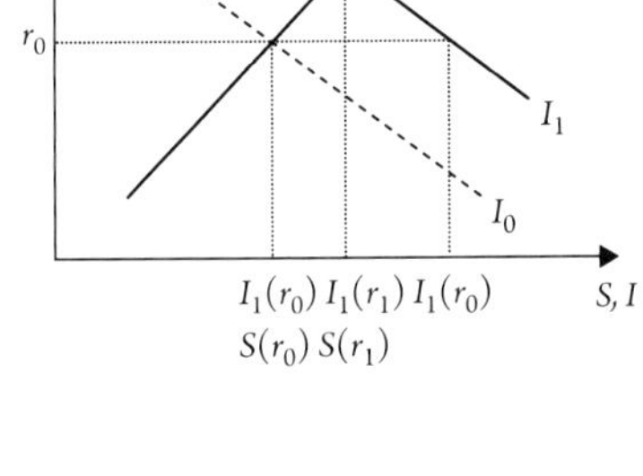

Figure 1.1.1

to a net addition to the supply of loanable funds provided by banks. The price level rises.

Conversely, in the event of a downward shift in the investment demand schedule, at the old rate of interest there will now exist an excess supply of commodities, corresponding to an excess demand for money, which, again in the absence of any countervailing action on the part of banks, will prompt the money rate to follow the natural rate downward pari passu. Compared with the *initial* equilibrium, consumption demand rises, while demand for capital goods falls, though that decline is tempered by the decline in the rate of interest, such that any immanent excess supply, and therefore deflationary pressure, is eliminated. The economy transitions to a new, lower growth path. As Wicksell thus concludes, "*If* it were possible to ascertain and specify the current value of the natural rate, it would be seen that any deviation of the actual money rate from this natural rate is connected with rising or falling prices according as the deviation is downward or upward."[13]

Will this inflation (or deflation) eventually come to an end? According to Wicksell, the answer is a provisional no. That is, "If the [money] rate of interest remains at a low level for a considerable period of time, its influence on prices must necessarily be *cumulative*."[14] Producers, it is true, will have to pay more for raw materials, wages, rents, et cetera, but will at the same time receive higher prices for their own products, meaning they find themselves in "precisely the same situation as before the rise in prices took place," and therefore able to pay the same rate of interest as before for the necessary credit. Assuming no revision of interest rate policy on the part of banks, producers will hence be in the same position as previously with respect to procuring additional raw materials, labor, and land. "As a consequence," Wicksell argues, "the demands of workers and landlords will be raised, and this will bring about a further rise in the price of consumption goods; and prices will continually rise higher and higher."[15] The entire process is a cumulative one.

Thus far, Wicksell's "cumulative process" would thereby seem to be a strictly nominal affair, with disequilibrium impacting only *absolute* prices. In fact, however, Wicksell saw the money–natural rate gap as redounding in a very real manner on *relative* prices. For a decline in the price of credit would tend to advantage producers of capital goods in particular, which suggests a diversion of labor and raw materials from the production of goods intended for consumption into investment. The consequent diminution in the quantity of consumption goods becoming annually available will then fall hardest upon fixed-income earners who, owing to the inflation of consumer goods prices, will be forced to consume less in *real* terms. In Wicksell's words, "The *real saving* which is necessary for . . . investment to be increased is in fact *enforced* at exactly the right moment on consumers as a whole; for a smaller quantity than usual of consumption goods is available for the consumption of the second year."[16] In conventional economic parlance, this effect is known as "forced saving."[17]

Nor is this "forced saving" effect a mere aside; it is in fact key to securing the identity between *ex post* saving and investment. Since, in Wicksell's schema, investment demand was initially satisfied by the banking system through the creation of credit, rather than the *ex ante* provision of saving, it is necessary that the real saving to constitute that investment be somehow mobilized elsewhere. The "enforcement" of liquid, or circulating, capital from the production of consumer into the production of investment goods furnishes that missing saving, such that, *ex post,* the equality of saving and investment still obtains.

In fact, because Wicksell has preserved the *ex post* saving-investment identity, the only occasion that can bring the cumulative process to a halt—and note that this means merely a halt to *further* price rises, *not* to a reversal of price increases that have already occurred—is if the elevated demand for money, in response to a higher nominal price level, impinges to an excessive extent on bank reserves. The problem is that Wicksell has thus far assumed a hypothetical pure credit economy, which means the reserve constraint is non-operative. To bring the cumulative process to a halt, Wicksell must therefore drop his initial assumption and instead assume an intermediate state of affairs between the two limiting cases of a pure barter and pure credit economy; in other words, a system of fractional-reserve banking, in which the quantity of credit circulating in the hands of the public is sufficiently larger than the available reserves of the banks that even a slight rise in prices might bring about a very significant contraction of bank reserves.[18] Then, in the event that banks do find reserves to be insufficient either to cover expected losses or else to meet official reserve requirements, the money rate will indeed have to rise. Essentially, the assumption of "outside" money is required to halt the cumulative process.

Wicksell's conclusion, therefore, is that "it is thus confidently to be expected that the Bank rate, or more generally the money rate of interest, will always coincide *eventually* with the natural capital rate, or rather that it is always *tending* to coincide with an ever-changing natural rate." The theoretical puzzle, however, is "whether this result is achieved with sufficient *rapidity* to prevent a continual rise in prices," in the event that the natural rate exceeds the money rate, "or to obviate a gradual fall in prices at times when the ... the money rate is left higher than the natural rate," an outcome that Wicksell insists "seems a priori very doubtful." Resolving this puzzle, however, "involves a survey of various complications which unfortunately requires a far more intimate insight ... than is at my disposal, particularly as the matter is partly associated with forces tending in contrary directions."[19] In other words, Wicksell, while endeavoring to explain how the cumulative process could continue for some time, was not inclined to venture too deeply into the theoretical morass of what might bring it to a halt, or even reverse it.

1.2. WICKSELL'S CAPITAL THEORY

The key claim of the cumulative process is thus that the burden of adjustment falls squarely upon the money rate of interest. This point cannot be overemphasized; not only does Leijonhufvud give it short shrift, but Wicksell's contemporary, David Davidson, even expressly dismissed it.[20] After all, Wicksell's conjecture that real savings may indeed be "enforced" via inflation would suggest that the cumulative process is by no means cumulative; capital accumulation achieved by means of forced saving—or any other form of saving, for that matter—must lead, assuming diminishing marginal productivity, to an inevitable decline in the natural rate of interest, thereby eliminating any incipient gap between money and natural rates.

To Davidson's critique, Wicksell's response was tentative, conceding provisionally that insofar as forced saving does permit the accumulation of capital, and production is "unable to absorb unlimited quantities of new capital without a reduction in net yield," then the cumulative process "might yet be arrested, unless the banks reduced their rate still further."[21] His response, in effect, was thus to partially evacuate his defense of forced saving, suggesting that the "counteracting forces" of real capital accumulation were merely "secondary factors" of the more fundamental axiom that the divergence of the rate of interest on real capital from that on loan credit will necessarily trigger price-level fluctuations, which may in actuality persist for some indeterminate amount of time.[22]

Wicksell's partial retreat from forced saving was, however, unwarranted, as the independence of the natural rate with respect to monetary changes was in fact buttressed by the theoretical framework erected in his *Interest and Prices* (1898). Indeed, this was the very *aim* of *Interest and Prices,* namely, to demonstrate the impossibility of credit institutions maintaining the lending rate indefinitely at any desired level, and rather that they "are obliged sooner or later, as a result of the operation on the money market of the forces of supply and demand, to come into line with the natural rate."[23] In other words, while the money rate of interest depends "in the first instance on the excess or scarcity of *money*," it is nonetheless the task of monetary economics to explain why and how "it is eventually determined by the excess or scarcity of *real capital*."[24] Recall that one of Wicksell's primary aims was precisely to reconcile the quantity theory with Gibson's Paradox; conceding that the money-rate tail could wag the natural-rate dog would require ditching the quantity theory entirely. A theoretical justification for the invariance of the natural rate with respect to money—rather than its mere tacit assumption—was thus fundamental to Wicksell's model.

Clearly, provision of such justification is difficult within a standard capital-theoretic framework; the realignment of the two rates—by one, the other, or both—is unavoidable with the combination of forced saving and diminishing marginal productivity. Separately from his monetary work, however, Wicksell had already recognized serious problems with the marginalist approach to capital theory. Essentially, whereas labor and land can each be measured in terms of its own *technical* unit (man-hours, acres, et cetera) heterogeneous capital in the aggregate must instead be expressed in value terms—how, otherwise, to sum a railroad and a sewing machine? Capital valuation is here unavoidable, meaning that a given capital stock must be measured either as the sum of inputs invested over time and capitalized at the rate of interest (i.e., cost of production, which requires time) or else as a stream of future output discounted by that rate of interest (i.e., revenue over time).[25] Both methods are equally valid.

Note, however, that with either approach, to calculate the marginal product of capital, that is, the natural rate, it is necessary to derive the value of capital goods from their cost of production or reproduction, or else from an expected future income stream, meaning, therefore, that "each particular capital-good is measured by a unit extraneous to itself."[26] But in this case, Wicksell observes, the "costs of production include *capital* and interest," while a future income stream must be discounted into present terms at the rate of interest, which requires that "we should, therefore, be arguing in a circle"; it is necessary to know the value of capital to calculate the rate of interest, but equally as requisite to know the interest rate to calculate the value of capital.[27] This is not an issue with land and labor because the addition of one more unit of land or labor does not alter the units in which land and labor are measured; bringing one more acre of land into production does not change the meaning of an acre, and the same with man-hours. But with capital, which must be measured in value terms, each additional unit of capital will indeed change the units in which capital is measured.

According to Wicksell, we can "escape from this difficulty" by adopting Austrian economist Eugen von Böhm-Bawerk's method of resolving all capital goods can into labor and land. That is, capital may be regarded as a mass of "saved-up" land and labor, weighted by date of input.[28] In this way, capital intensity refers not precisely to the physical stock of capital goods in existence per se but rather to the average interval of time for which the land and labor embodied in that stock have been invested, Böhm-Bawerk's "average period of production." The productivity of capital is thus a function of what Wicksell, following Böhm-Bawerk, calls the "*time-element* in production"; land and labor are rendered more productive the longer they are invested.[29] It is then possible to define the natural rate of interest on capital as the marginal productivity of extending the length of time for which original factors are invested; that is, the natural rate is the rate of return on the last increment of capital, where capital is a mass of saved-up land and labor.

Wicksell's Böhm-Bawerkian conception of capital is closely bound up with his construction of the cumulative process. For, he notes, "The enterprises which par excellence are in a position to draw labour and land to themselves as a result of an actual or virtual easing in the terms of credit are those for which the period of investment of capital is relatively long," as wages and rents will have relatively less impact on "longer" production processes than on shorter ones. "Production," Wicksell concludes, "will consequently tend to be diverted in such a way as to increase the average length of the period of investment of capital, and liquid capital will tend to be converted into fixed capital."[30] In other words, a money rate of interest below the natural rate will tend not simply to raise investment but in particular to raise investment in projects of exceptionally long gestation.

Moreover, Wicksell contends, there exists an elemental difference between liquid and fixed capital, or capital involving an especially lengthy period of production. The difference is that capital goods of exceptional durability, though they possess "the attributes of capital and of other capital goods," their role in production in fact "comes nearest to that played by *land*." Wicksell proposes, therefore, "that they shall be regarded, not as capital goods, but as a kind of 'rent-earning goods,' which ... earn for their owners a certain rent (analogous to the rent of land)."[31] Though these goods may not constitute capital "in the narrow sense of the word," they nonetheless require continued investment of liquid capital in order to be maintained undiminished, such that the land and labor applied to them "can on each occasion be regarded as representing a new investment of capital."[32]

Consider, therefore, the cumulative process in the light of Böhm-Bawerkian capital theory. As before, a relative decline in the money rate of interest serves to stimulate investment, but particularly investment in "those enterprises which employ 'more capital,' i.e. in which the period of investment is longer than elsewhere." The short-run price-elasticity of supply of these "rent-earning" capital goods being essentially zero, competition among entrepreneurs for productive factors will tend to raise the relative price of these goods compared to capital of notably less durability, which means that "available original factors of production could be employed in a longer, and therefore more productive, process."[33] But this increased capital investment, and the consequent upward pressure on wages and rents, while we might expect it to "rapidly depress the rate of interest," owing to the property of diminishing marginal productivity, is not, Wicksell insists, "decisive." The reason is that capital goods of exceptional durability in fact "take part in the rise enjoyed by wages and rents."[34,35] Profits on fixed capital, in other words, should increase.

But while we might expect the upward pressure on wages and rents to squeeze the rate of profit on "capital in the narrow sense," this tendency will be counteracted by the effect of a lower supply of liquid capital as more is in essence "frozen" in the form of investment in longer-duration goods. That is, the diversion of liquid capital into the production of more durable capital goods must, in conditions of full employment and *in the absence of* prior saving, involve a reduction in immediately available liquid capital, or, what is the same thing, a reduction in the "wages-and-rent fund" from which wages and rent are advanced from previously saved-up land and labor.[36,37] Essentially, there is a seesaw effect at work between "rent-earning" capital goods and capital goods "in the narrow sense," with the rate of return first on one and then the other rising at the other's expense, such that the overall natural rate of interest on capital *in the aggregate* will not decline as the cumulative process proceeds.[38]

The bottom line, then, according to Wicksell, is that the natural rate *cannot* be relied upon to bear the burden of adjustment to a maladjustment that is *monetary* in origin. A fall in the natural rate would imply an increase in the supply of *real* capital—a state of affairs which Wicksell, still committed to the quantity theory as a long-run proposition, was unwilling to countenance. As it was, he was willing to concede that the proposition "that a lowering of the loan rate must also depress the real rate so that the difference between them is more leveled out and thus the stimulus to a continued rise in prices is eliminated.... cannot be entirely rejected." Given, however, that, ceteris paribus, a declining real rate "unconditionally demands new real capital, i.e. increased saving," Wicksell's conclusion was that the addition to real capital contributed by forced saving would have, therefore, to outweigh not only the *decrease* in voluntary saving owing to a lower rate of interest, but also the fact that competition between fixed and circulating capital would tend to keep the natural rate elevated.[39]

1.3. THE WICKSELL CONNECTION

Leijonhufvud is entirely correct to classify the saving-investment approach as fundamental to Wicksellian natural rate theory. Wicksell's cumulative process is predicated upon the notion that the interest rate cannot always be relied upon to coordinate the separate decisions to save and invest. Decades of neo-Walrasian general equilibrium theorizing have conditioned economists to overlook this point. But the loanable funds story is only half of the Wicksell connection. The cumulative price process in Wicksell's loanable funds analysis depends upon the *persistence* of the divergence between the money and natural rates, or, more precisely, upon the burden of adjustment resting solely and strictly upon the money rate. Invariance of the natural rate with respect to monetary maladjustments must therefore, for Wicksell's cumulative process to indeed be cumulative, be analytically justified. Here, his use of Böhm-Bawerk's longitudinal approach to capital is crucial; otherwise, Wicksell's natural rate is left hanging.[40]

Yet the natural rate itself is not entirely free of further complications. Indeed, Wicksell admits that the natural rate is a rather "vague" conception, with its exact determination, even from a purely theoretical perspective, involving "great difficulties."[41] The paramount dilemma, he realized, was that his "assumption that the average period of investment is independent of the rate of interest (i.e. of simple interest) only applies, strictly speaking, where several different capital investments relate to one and the same future act of consumption." In other words, the average period of production is independent of the interest rate only if there is no durable capital, namely, only if production is of the simple continuous-input—point-output type. But even then, independence obtains only with the assumption of simple interest. Absent these exceptionally restrictive assumptions, we are, as Wicksell put it, arguing in a circle, escape from which would require "paying simultaneous regard" to all conditions of production, "in the manner first demonstrated very clearly by Léon Walras" (a prescient point, as we shall later see).[42]

The "difficulty" pertaining to this circularity is the fact that capital values will consequently vary not only on the basis of capital scarcity and the technical properties of the marginal product of capital but also on relative input prices (in a two-factor model with labor and capital, this means the wage and interest rates). Thus we have "price Wicksell effects," which are the result of capitalizing or revaluing the same physical stock of capital as the wage rate and rate of interest assume different values; as well as "real Wicksell effects," which refer to changes in production technique induced by changes in the wage and interest rates, and thus involve differences in the actual physical stock of capital goods.[43,44] While thus acknowledging that the unambiguous coincidence of the natural rate of interest with the "marginal productivity of waiting" is applicable only "on certain abstract assumptions," and even then "only as a mathematical concept, without direct physical or psychic significance," Wicksell insists nonetheless that it should be retained "as a concise general principle, reflecting the essence of productive capital," namely, time[45]

Wicksell's own cumulative process, however, is not immune to price and real Wicksell effects. He even concedes that "actually the complications are greater," since "we have been making the implicit assumption that the relative values of commodities in exchange remain unaltered. But they are, of course, affected by the change in the conditions of production, and they in their turn exert an influence on the conditions of production."[46] In other words, since capital is measured in units extraneous to itself, each additional increment of value capital will change the relative values of the inputs in which capital is measured, and will thus alter the relative profitability of different production processes. A theoretically hermetic model of the cumulative process would thus have to account for the complicating factor of variable relative prices. Indeed, Wicksell himself was aware of this shortcoming, writing that "it would be necessary for the sake of completeness to consider the influence exerted by all these various changes on capital structure itself."[47] While he adroitly opted to ignore such complications, Wicksell effects nonetheless constitute a key element of our Wicksell connection.

Where, then, does this leave us with respect to the Wicksell "connection"? The divergence of the natural from the money rate of interest (or vice versa) constitutes the mainspring of disequilibrium, allowing investment demand to deviate, indefinitely, from the supply of saving. But this is only possible because Wicksell assumes a sequential lag in prices, whereby savings are in effect "forced" from consumers via consumer price inflation. While this forced saving complicates the cumulativeness of the process, Wicksell tentatively plugs the theoretical gap by retooling capital theory.

Leijonhufvud sums up Wicksell by saying that "the process would go on cumulatively as long as the market rate is kept below natural rate."[48] That this is so, however, owes precisely to Wicksell's reliance on Austrian capital theory, in which changes in credit operate upon a heterogeneous time structure of production. Without his temporal distinction between "rent-earning" capital and capital "in the narrow sense," Wicksell would be unable to assert, as he does, that "in an elastic monetary system, where there is only a small reaction against an alteration in prices, a fairly constant difference between the two rates of interest could be maintained for a long time, and the effect on prices might be considerable."[49] The burden of adjustment, as it were, rests solely and squarely upon the shoulders of the *money* rate of interest.

The Wicksellian link, as a genealogical concept, is thus manifestly twofold, occupying both monetary and real dimensions, meaning any discussion of Wicksell's cumulative process that omits mention of Böhm-Bawerkian capital theory ignores fundamentally the very theoretical foundations upon which the natural rate concept was predicated, depriving the natural rate of its attractive force and rendering the saving-investment approach a distinctly nominal affair. What is *lacking* in the Wicksell link is precisely what Wicksell himself failed to pin down, namely, a measure of capital intensity, independent of changes in relative prices, as it responds to changes in the rate of interest, as well as an account of relative price changes over the course of the cumulative process.

Moreover, we should be careful to note that Wicksell himself did not see his cumulative process as an explanation of the business *cycle*. While acknowledging that "changes in the purchasing power of money, caused by credit policy," are "intimately bound up" with the business cycle, "above all by giving rise to crises," he nonetheless contended that "yet it does not seem essential to assume that there is, by the nature of things, any necessary connection between these two phenomena." Rather, according to Wicksell, the primary and sufficient cause of the business cycle is in the inability of "technical and commercial progress" to proceed as smoothly as the growth in human wants and needs. In other words, supply-side technical change will inevitably fluctuate around the more steady growth in consumer demand. To be sure, if banks sufficiently raised or lowered their interest rates as technical progress (and thus the return on capital) exceeds or falls short of consumers' willingness to provide real savings, "then the price level would probably remain stable," and, "under such circumstances the chief crises-causing factor would probably have disappeared." What remained would then be "only a quiet wave movement" between periods of accelerated fixed capital formation, and periods of increased accumulation of liquid stocks.[50] Prudent credit policy, therefore, while it might not eliminate business fluctuations, could at least prevent them from growing too violent.

Thus, for Wicksell, the cumulative process is not so much a cause of the business cycle, as it is symptomatic of the tendency, inherent in the very nature of a modern monetary economy, to react in an oscillatory manner to irregular real shocks. Accordingly likening the "indifferent equilibrium" of the general price level in a monetary system of high elasticity to that of a ball or cylinder on a horizontal plane, Wicksell suggests that by inertia and friction it will remain stationary unless forces "of sufficient strength" drive it from its position of initial equilibrium. In this case, though it will have no tendency to reassume its initial position, once the forces which set it in motion—namely, the difference between the natural and money rates of interest—cease to operate, the price level, like the cylinder, will remain in a new and likewise indifferent equilibrium position. To this inertial instability, however, Wicksell contrasts the comparative stability of relative prices, which he likens to a pendulum, or ball at the bottom of a bowl; "Every movement away from the position of equilibrium sets forces into operation—on a scale that increases with the extent of the movement—which tend to restore the system to its original position, and actually succeed in doing so, though some oscillations may intervene."[51] The key questions arising, then, are the relative strengths of these two opposing forces, and whether and to what extent, or under what conditions, deviation-counteraction by one can be relied upon to attenuate deviation-amplification by the other.

NOTES

1. Axel Leijonhufvud, "The Wicksell Connection: Variations on a Theme," in *Information and Coordination: Essays in Macroeconomic Theory* (New York: Oxford University Press, 1981), 131.
2. Ibid., 134.
3. G.L.S. Shackle, foreword to Knut Wicksell, *Value, Capital, and Rent*, trans. S.H. Frowein (1893; reprint, London: George Allen & Unwin, 1954), 7.
4. Don Patinkin, "Wicksell's 'Cumulative Process,'" *Economic Journal* 62 (1952): 836.
5. Joan Robinson, *The Accumulation of Capital*, 3d ed. (1956; reprint, London: Palgrave Macmillan, 1969), 396.
6. Axel Leijonhufvud, *On Keynesian Economics and the Economics of Keynes: A Study in Monetary Theory* (New York: Oxford University Press, 1968), 276.
7. Knut Wicksell, *Interest and Prices: A Study of the Causes Regulating the Value of Money*, trans. R. F. Kahn (1898; reprint, London: Macmillan, 1936), 38–50.
8. Wicksell occasionally refers interchangeably to the "natural" rate also as the "real" or "capital" rate, and the "money" rate also as the "bank" or "market" rate. We will use simply "natural" and "money."
9. Wicksell, *Interest and Prices*, 104.
10. Knut Wicksell, *Lectures on Political Economy*, vol. 2, *Money*, ed. Lional Robins, trans. E. Classen (1906; reprint, London: Routledge and Kegan Paul, 1935), 204.
11. Wicksell, *Interest and Prices*, 119.
12. Ibid., 106. Among these "thousand and one things," the natural rate depends on "the efficiency of production, on the available amount of fixed and liquid capital, on the supply of labour and land."

13. Ibid., 107 (emphasis added).
14. Ibid., 95 (emphasis in original).
15. Ibid.
16. Ibid., 149, 155–156.
17. For a history of the doctrine of forced saving, see F. A. Hayek, "A Note on the Development of the Doctrine of 'Forced Saving,'" *Quarterly Journal of Economics* 47 (1932): 123–133; Fritz Machlup, "Forced or Induced Saving: An Exploration into Its Synonyms and Homonyms," *Review of Economic Statistics* 25 (1943): 26–39.
18. Wicksell, *Interest and Prices*, 114.
19. Ibid., 117.
20. Leijonhufvud, "The Wicksell Connection," 151–164; David Davidson, "Om stabiliseringen af penningens värde" ("Concerning Stabilization of the Value of Money"), *Ekonomisk Tidskrift* 11, häft 1 (1909): 1–25. Wicksell's reply: K. Wicksell, "Penningränta och varupris" ("The Money Rate of Interest and Commodity Prices"), *Ekonomisk Tidskrift* 11, häft 2 (1909): 61–66. Davidson's rejoinder: D. Davidson, "Penningränta och varupris: Replik (till Wicksell)" ("The Money Rate of Interest and Commodity Prices: Reply [to Wicksell]"), *Ekonomisk Tidskrift* 11, häft 2 (1909): 67–68.
21. Wicksell, *Lectures*, 2:199.
22. Ibid., 200.
23. Wicksell, *Interest and Prices*, 108.
24. Emphasis in original. Wicksell further adds that "it is thus confidently to be expected that the Bank rate, or more generally the money rate of interest, will always coincide eventually with the natural capital rate, or rather that it is always tending to coincide with an ever-changing natural rate." The key question, therefore, is "whether this result is achieved with sufficient rapidity to prevent a continual rise in prices at times when the capital rate is rising (so that the money rate is left below the natural rate), or to obviate a gradual fall in prices at times when the capital rate is falling (and consequently the money rate is left higher than the natural rate)," a result that Wicksell concludes "seems a priori very doubtful." Ibid., 108, 117.
25. Alternatively, if production is (more realistically) characterized by continuous input and continuous output, then the value of a capital asset can be calculated as the integral of the difference between the input and output functions of that asset for the duration of its life.
26. Knut Wicksell, *Lectures on Political Economy*, vol. 1, *General Theory*, ed. Lional Robins, trans. E. Classen (1901; reprint, London: Routledge and Kegan Paul, 1935), 149.
27. Ibid.
28. This continuous-input—point-output approach is, as we will see in subsequent chapters, a simplification that conveniently avoids certain theoretical

problems associated with durable capital. Wicksell was certainly aware that the continuous-input—point-output model was an abstraction from reality. He notes that "this longitudinal section... actually extends indefinitely in time in both directions. This indefiniteness, however, is of no practical importance, since the major portion lies between finite limits." Thus, "the indirect demand for the factors of production from the consumers side becomes a mere metaphor, and we also cease to take capital-goods into consideration; adopting the scheme of Jevons and Böhm-Bawerk, everything is resolved into a continuous production directed towards the future." Ibid., 237.

29. Wicksell further adds that the importance of the time element in production "was never properly appreciated by Walras and his school." Ibid., 150, 171.
30. Wicksell, *Interest and Prices*, 149.
31. Wicksell's term is "Rentengüter." He suggests that "examples are provided by houses, streets, railways, canals, certain improvements in land, certain kinds of machines." Ibid., 126. See also Wicksell, *Lectures*, 1:186–187, 237.
32. Capital "in the narrow sense of the word," i.e., liquid capital, would then refer to "tools, machines, improvements in land, etc., of relatively *low* durability (though the dividing line has to be drawn somewhat arbitrarily), furthermore raw materials and semi-manufactured products, and finally stocks of finished consumption goods." Wicksell, *Interest and Prices*, 126–127.
33. Ibid., 143–144.
34. Ibid., 132–133.
35. A further reason offered by Wicksell against the natural rate bearing the burden of adjustment is that "the quantity of *durable* capital goods ('rent-earning goods') is in general capable of expansion." That is to say, fixed plant and land improvements are rarely utilized to their full capacity, which means that in the face of easy credit, the mobilization of slack capacity may allow fixed-capital investment to proceed some time before productivity is appreciably diminished. Ibid., 134. See also Wicksell, *Lectures*, 1:186. This entire argument is more fully analyzed in Olivier Jenn-Treyer, "The 'Wicksell Connection' and the Austrian Theory of Capital: Which Connections?" in *Evolution of the Market Process: Austrian and Swedish Economics*, ed. M. Bellet, S. Gloria-Palermo, and A. Zaouche (London: Routledge, 2004), 170–196.
36. Wicksell, *Interest and Prices*, 133–134.
37. Wicksell essentially adhered to a more sophisticated version of the old "wages fund" model of the Classical economists, preferring instead the notion of a "wages-and-rent fund" from which income would be advanced to labor, land, and "rent-earning" capital goods. Suppose, for example, a producer advances wages (l_1) and rents (r_1) to produce a machine of low durability in year 1. In year 2, a second producer purchases the machine and pays in advance l_2 and r_2 to produce a specific quantity of raw materials, since the machine is

assumed to wear out by the end of year 2. In year 3, a third producer will then advance l_3 and r_3 to produce a certain quantity of final goods, to be sold at the end of the year. We thus have a complete production process of fixed capital, circulating capital, and final output, which, expressed in wage and rent units, amounts to:

$$(l_1+l_2+l_3)+(r_1+r_2+r_3)=l+r=k$$

From this, Wicksell calculates average investment periods for wages, t_l, and rent, t_r:

$$\begin{cases} \dfrac{3l_1+2l_2+l_3}{l}=t_l \\ \dfrac{3r_1+2r_2+r_3}{r}=t_r \end{cases}$$

For the entire capital stock, the average investment period is thus:

$$\frac{3(l_1+r_1)+2(l_2+r_2)+(l_3+r_3)}{l+r}=\frac{l\cdot t_l+r\cdot t_r}{k}=t$$

Aggregating the k's from each individual industry, we obtain $K=\sum k$; total capital is equal to the total value of consumer goods invested at any time in the form of capital. The average period of investment of K is then:

$$T=\frac{\sum k\cdot t}{\sum k}$$

The ratio K/T Wicksell calls the "annual wages-and-rent fund," representing the quantity of capital that is freed up each year from the process of production. K, liquid or circulating capital, is thus the "aggregate wages-and-rent fund."

He then derives the following "approximately true" equation relating the amount of labor (A) and available land (B) to total circulating capital:

$$(A\cdot l+B\cdot r)\cdot T=K$$

The equation satisfies the conditions of full employment at the macro level; that is, it states that all original factors of production, land and labor, are employed within the structure of production. More important, however, Wicksell argues that "$B\cdot r$ really stands for the sum of all 'rent-earning goods,' each measured in terms of its own unit of measure...and multiplied by the corresponding rent." He thus decouples fixed and circulating capital.

Wicksell, *Interest and Prices,* 129–131. See also Jenn-Treyer, "The 'Wicksell Connection,'" 188–189.

38. Jenn-Treyer, "The 'Wicksell Connection,'" 188–189.
39. Wicksell, *Lectures,* 2: 198–199.
40. Wicksell himself poses the choice in these terms, noting that "we can *either* adopt Walras' method of taking a *cross-section* through social production at a moment of time.... *Or else* we can refer everything back to the original factors of production in conjunction with waiting (or preferably time). Here we take a *longitudinal section* instead." Wicksell, *Lectures,* 1:236–237, 226–227. See also Wicksell, *Interest and Prices,* 125–126.
41. Wicksell, *Interest and Prices,* 120.
42. Ibid., 132.
43. Suppose output is a function of capital and labor. If total output is exhausted by factor remuneration, then output per head, q, is

$$q = rk + w$$

where r is the rate of profit, and k and w capital per head and the wage rate, respectively. In long-run equilibrium, a variation in the rate of profit must entail a simultaneous adjustment of the wage rate, output, and capital per head. The variation in the value of capital can thus be expressed by the differential:

$$dk = \frac{1}{r}(dq - kdr - dw)$$

Accordingly, the marginal productivity of capital is not equal to the rate of profits, but rather:

$$\frac{dq}{dk} = r + k\frac{dr}{dk} + \frac{dw}{dk}$$

We can also break down our equation for variation in the value of capital to obtain:

$$dk = \frac{1}{r}dq - \frac{k}{r}dr - \frac{1}{r}dw$$

The first term of this equation may be interpreted as the capitalized value of physical productivity and corresponds to the "real Wicksell effect." The other two terms correspond to revaluation effects of the same physical stock, a.k.a. "price Wicksell effects." According to the sign of dk/dw (i.e., contrary to the sign of dk/dr), the price Wicksell effect will be positive or negative. See G. C. Harcourt, *Some Cambridge Controversies in the Theory of Capital* (Cambridge: Cambridge University Press, 1972), 40–42.

44. Wicksell, *Lectures,* 1:178–180. For more on Wicksell effects, see M. Blaug, *Economic Theory in Retrospect,* 3d ed. (Cambridge: Cambridge University Press, 1978), 591–592; Avi J. Cohen and G. C. Harcourt, "Retrospectives: Whatever Happened to the Cambridge Capital Theory Controversies?," *Journal of Economic Perspectives* 17 (2003): 199–214; G. C. Harcourt, "Some Cambridge Controversies in the Theory of Capital," *Journal of Economic Literature* 7 (1969): 369–405.
45. Wicksell, *Lectures,* 1:184.
46. Wicksell, *Interest and Prices,* 132. Wicksell adds that "the only scientific method of dealing with the problem consists in paying *simultaneous* regard to all these factors, in the manner first demonstrated very clearly by Léon Walras." This approach, however, forswears any aspirations toward deducing causality, which was the aim of Wicksell's sequential analysis.
47. Ibid., 134.
48. Leijonhufvud, "The Wicksell Connection," 164.
49. Wicksell, *Interest and Prices,* 110.
50. Wicksell, *Lectures,* 2: 211–213.
51. Ibid., 196–197. See also Wicksell, *Interest and Prices,* 100–101.

Chapter 2

A Treatise versus *Prices and Production*

In the first iteration of the Wicksell connection, Wicksell's own, there were two fundamental propositions: first, a divergence between two rates of interest, "money" and "natural," induces a cumulative rise in prices that, second, will only be halted if and when, due to the exhaustion of reserves ("outside" money), banks are compelled to raise the interest rate at which they extend loans. This second proposition followed from Wicksell's hypothesis that attendant to the cumulative process is a maturation of liquid into durable capital, as the lower market rate of interest engenders a tendency toward a "lengthening" of the average period of production, with the result that the natural rate of interest cannot be relied upon to restore equality between the two rates. Accompanying these two essentials of the Wicksell "connection," however, were two critical theoretical shortcomings: first, Wicksell (admittedly) fails to account for relative price changes during the course of the cumulative process and, second, the capital-theoretic foundations of his natural rate are flawed; outside of a one-commodity world, the natural rate is indefinable.

As noted in chapter 1, there is nothing in Wicksell's framework that explicitly aspires to a theory of the credit *cycle*. The cumulative process either continues indefinitely or is choked off by bank tightening. In our second iteration of the Wicksell connection, however, Keynes and Hayek both attempt to translate Wicksell's cumulative process into a cyclical phenomenon: why an inflationary cumulative process must ultimately be self-reversing (though Keynes devoted most of his attention to the reverse case of a deflationary cumulative process).[1] In so doing, Keynes's *A Treatise on Money* (1930) and Hayek's *Prices and Production* (1931) integrate the role of relative prices fundamentally into the cumulative process and, indeed, posit *changes* in relative prices as the sine qua non of the business cycle. The market–natural rate distinction remains, as does the potential divergence of saving and investment and the forced saving mechanism. Ultimately, disequilibrium in the two models stems from an unresolved conflict within the structure of production, a rivalry between producers of consumer and investment goods corresponding strictly to the failure of adjustment between saving and investment. In this, the Wicksellian two-rates framework is decisive, constituting a disequilibrating trip wire within capital markets that touches off a progressive sequence of ultimately re-equilibrating secular price changes.

The first section of this chapter reconstructs the basic model of Keynes's *Treatise on Money*, teasing out, in particular, the elements of the Wicksell connection in Keynes's "fundamental equations." Though the primary concern of *A Treatise* is deflation, here we focus on Keynes's account of the inflationary phase of the business cycle, so as to more readily contrast his model with those of Hayek and Wicksell. In the second section, we examine Hayek's *Prices and Production* model, emphasizing especially Hayek's elaboration of Austro-Wicksellian capital theory. The chapter concludes by recapitulating the shared Wicksellian framework driving both models.

2.1. *A TREATISE ON MONEY*

The crux of the *Treatise* model is embodied in what Keynes calls the "fundamental equations," linking the price level to factor earnings and, crucially, the discrepancy between saving and investment. He begins by defining aggregate output (O) as the sum of consumption goods (R) and investment goods (C). That is,

$$O = R + C$$

Given respective price levels, P and P,′ the value of aggregate output is thus:

$$\pi O = PR + P'C$$

where π denotes the general price level. From here, Keynes casts a dizzying web of algebraic manipulations, attempting to pack a formulaic conglomeration into the portmanteau of just two equations.[2,3] The basic premise is that the value of aggregate production is simply the sum of the two sectors, consumer and investment, the latter being equal to the market value of current investment-good output (i.e., $P'C = I$).[4] Simplifying, we get:

$$\pi O = PR + I \qquad (2.1.1)$$

Given total nominal output, we can then define the equilibrium condition for businesses as:

$$\pi O = E + Q \qquad (2.1.2)$$

That is, total revenue, πO, is the sum of "normal" earnings of the factors of production (earnings exclusive of short-term variations), E, and "windfall," or exceptional, profits or losses, Q. The equilibrium condition for households is then:

$$E = PR + S \qquad (2.1.3)$$

meaning households distribute remunerated earnings between consumption and saving (factor income not consumed). Equations 2.1.1 and 2.1.3 thus yield what Keynes calls the "Second Fundamental Equation":

$$\pi = \frac{E}{O} + \frac{I - S}{O}$$

Explicitly, the aggregate price level, π, is determined by the relative shares of output owing to normal factor earnings and windfall profits.

Keynes then also derives an analogous equation representing the price level of consumer goods specifically. Taking equation 2.1.3, we see that the price level of consumption goods is:

$$P = \frac{E - S}{R} \tag{2.1.4}$$

If we then disaggregate normal earnings into income earned from the production of consumption goods, E', and income earned from the production of investment goods, I', we can rewrite equation 2.1.4 in the form:

$$P = \frac{E'}{R} + \frac{I' - S}{R}$$

Since Keynes assumes the physical unit of production to be the same for consumption as for investment goods, the unit production cost of consumption goods, E'/R, is equal to that of total output, E/O, meaning equation 2.1.4 further reduces to:

$$P = \frac{E}{O} + \frac{I' - S}{R}$$

This is the "First Fundamental Equation."

From the two fundamental equations, we can see that the price level of consumption goods (P) may differ from the overall price level (π) for two reasons: the value of new investment goods differs from their cost of production (i.e., $I \neq I'$), and/or aggregate real output (O) differs from real consumption-good output (R).[5] In other words, relative price changes arise from changes in the value of new investment goods relative to their production cost, as well as from shifts in the composition of output. The fundamental equations accordingly allow Keynes to correlate market discoordination with fluctuations in relative price levels, which, according to Allan Meltzer, the Keynes of *A Treatise* considered "central" to the theory of the business cycle.[6] The "mainspring of change" in the fundamental equations is thus Keynes's "windfall profit," with windfall profits (or losses) resulting from the divergence of the market values of capital and consumer goods from their "normal" or "long-period" supply prices, or, equivalently, from "normal" factor earnings.[7] In other words, windfall profits are merely the excess of revenue over costs, such that profit in the production of consumption goods, Q_1, is $Q_1 = PR - E'$, or $Q_1 = E' + I' - S - E' = I' - S$, and profit on investment goods, Q_2, is $Q_2 = I - I'$. Total profits are then simply the sum of profits in each sector, that is, $Q = Q_1 + Q_2 = I' - S + I - I' = I - S$.[8] The presence of windfall profits or losses, therefore, corresponds strictly to a disparity between investment and saving.

This protracted exercise has been necessary in order to draw out the Wicksell connection from Keynes's labyrinth of algebraic identities. Hints of that connection should already be detected in the decisive role played by a saving-investment gap in the fundamental equations. The Wicksellian influence penetrates much deeper into the fundamental equations, however, as, for Keynes, the incipient trigger of that decisive gap between savings and investment is a hypothetical incongruence between a "market" and "natural" rate of interest. In *A Treatise*, the latter is, as per Wicksell, "the rate at which saving and the value of investment are exactly balanced, so the price level of output as a whole...exactly corresponds to the money-rate of efficiency-earnings of the Factors of Production."[9] In other words, it is the rate that will simultaneously secure the equality of saving and investment and stabilize overall prices at a level consistent with "normal" earnings. The market rate is then simply the rate "which actually prevails" in the economy, and is equivalent to Wicksell's money rate.[10]

Insofar as the financial system transmits to investors the same quantity of loanable funds as that part of savings that is not directly invested, but rather converted into savings deposits, an autonomous rise in the rate of saving should correspond to a fall in the natural rate of interest. As banks accordingly make available more credit at lower cost to entrepreneurs for the purpose of investment, investment should rise pari passu. We can observe as much in the fundamental equations; given normal earnings, a rise in savings must be accompanied by a fall in the price of consumption goods.[11] At the same time, with zero interference on the part of financiers, a lower rate of interest will immediately raise the value of investment-good output, $P'C$, which means, since $P'C = I$, that investment demand will rise.[12] The situation is thus that there will be windfall losses in the consumption goods sector ($Q_1 = I' - S < 0$), windfall profits in the investment goods sector ($Q_2 = I - I' > 0$), and zero profits in the aggregate ($Q = I - S = 0$).[13] Eventually, higher factor incomes in the investment goods sector (I' rises) will eliminate any sectoral windfall profits or losses, and it will once again be the case that $Q = Q_1 = Q_2 = 0$, with money expenditure having merely been shifted between the two sectors.

In Keynes's schema, as in Wicksell's, problems arise only if the financial system extends as investible funds more or less than the volume of total savings, or, what is the same thing, if the market rate of interest differs from the natural rate. Keynes notes that "the higher the rate of interest, the lower, other things being equal, will be the value of capital goods." Consequently, as the rate of interest rises, "P' will tend to fall, which will lower the rate of profit on the production of capital-goods, which will be a deterrent to new investment."[14] On the other hand, the rate of saving is "stimulated by a high rate of interest," meaning, ceteris paribus, an increase in the rate of interest will tend to lower the rate of investment relative to the rate of saving.[15] Or, equivalently, the second terms in the fundamental equations will turn negative, implying a decline in both consumer and aggregate price levels. Thus, *if* a "change in the market-rate does *not* exactly correspond to a change in the natural rate... the decline in the rate of investment will cause a fall in P additional to any fall caused by the increase of savings," such that we have a fall in both P' and P, with consequent downward pressure on nominal output.[16]

It is helpful here to revisit figure 1.1.1.[17] Suppose, for example, that the economy begins in equilibrium, with the market rate equal to the natural rate at r_0, such that $S(r_0) = I_0(r_0)$ and $Q = Q_1 = Q_2 = 0$, as shown in figure 2.2.1. A rise in the natural rate, from r_0 to r_1, will be accompanied by an outward shift of the investment demand schedule, from I_0 to I_1, consistent with an autonomous increase in the value of investment goods.[18] The immediate impact is an excess demand for commodities at the original rate of interest, in the amount of $I_1(r_0) - S(r_0)$, corresponding to an excess flow supply of new securities. Businesses intend to float securities at the rate $I_1(r_0)$, while the household sector intends to accumulate income-bearing assets only at the rate $S(r_0)$. This places downward pressure on securities prices, as businesses are forced to accept lower bids on new securities, thereby pushing up the market rate.[19] Assuming full information and the absence of financial market rigidities, the market rate would immediately rise to equality with the new natural rate. Windfall profits and losses may still exist in the investment and

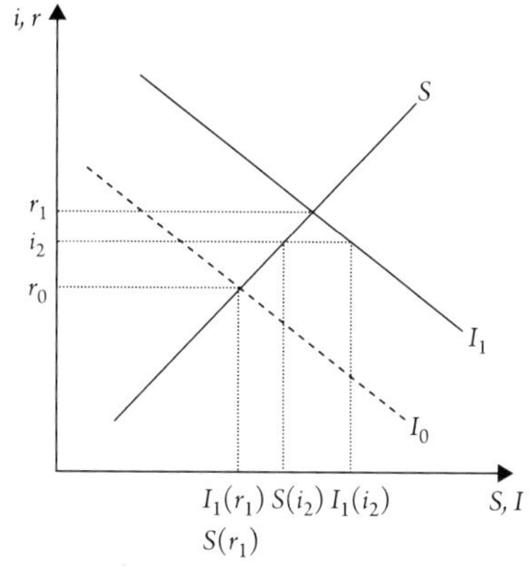

Figure 2.1.1

consumption-goods sectors, respectively, but so long as the market rate hones in on the "right" rate, aggregate windfall profits will be nil and prices will tend toward a uniform level consistent with normal earnings in both consumption- and investment-goods sectors.[20]

In Keynes's view, however, speculation steps into the role filled by Wicksell's banks in holding up adjustment at the "wrong" rate. Accustomed to asset yields at the level of r_0, speculators become bullish as securities prices trend downward, anticipating yields to revert to the old natural rate. At i_2, for example, bulls are buying "old" securities from savers in the amount of $I_1(i_2) - S(i_2)$ and releasing idle cash into active circulation at the corresponding flow rate. In essence, the stickiness of the market rate raises the relative return of real to monetary assets, with speculators substituting income-earning securities for cash.[21] The securities market clears, even though the market rate is stuck below the natural rate, meaning entrepreneurs earn windfall profits of $I_1(i_2) - S(i_2)$. Owing to the imperfect adjustment of the market rate, the economy faces an excess demand for commodities, matched by an excess flow supply of cash, equal to Q.[22]

Conversely, we might consider the consequences of an autonomous decline in the natural rate. Such a fall will be accompanied by an inward shift of the investment demand schedule, with the immediate impact being an excess supply of commodities at the original rate of interest, corresponding to an excess flow demand for new securities. Businesses intend to float securities at a rate determined by the intersection of the new, lower investment demand schedule with the old rate of interest, while the household sector intends to accumulate income-bearing assets at the old rate, along their original saving supply schedule.[23] This places upward pressure on securities prices, as savers bid up new securities, thereby pushing down yields and the money rate. Again, analogously to the inflationary case, if we assume full information and the absence of financial market rigidities, the money rate will immediately fall to equality with the new natural rate.

However, with the deflationary as with the inflationary scenario, speculation can hold up adjustment at the "wrong" rate. Accustomed to asset yields at their initial level, speculators become bearish as securities prices trend upward, anticipating yields to revert to the old natural rate. At intermediate rates of interest, bears are offloading "old" securities onto savers in the amount of the excess of saving over investment, and absorbing idle cash from active circulation at the equivalent rate.[24] In this case, the stickiness of the money rate raises the relative return of monetary to real assets, with speculators substituting cash for income-earning securities. Once again, the securities market clears, despite the fact that the money rate is stuck above the natural rate, meaning entrepreneurs earn windfall losses. The economy faces an excess supply of commodities, matched by an excess demand for cash balances.[25] As in Wicksell's story, the result is cumulative deflation.

Nonetheless, Keynes's variant of the Wicksellian cumulative process is patently re-equilibrating. To preserve the inflationary disequilibrium status quo at the "wrong" rate of interest, Keynes's bullish speculators would have to persist in divesting cash assets and replacing them with low-yield securities, meaning they must persist in the expectation that the relative price level of investment goods will rise, even in the face of relentless pressure on consumer goods prices to rise pari passu.[26] At i_2, insofar as factor remuneration is nominally rigid, windfall profits emerge in the production of *both* investment *and* consumer goods: the market value of current investment-good output, *I*, exceeds the cost of new capital goods, *I'*, and *I'* exceeds the supply of savings, *S*, the latter of which has declined in response to a lower rate of interest.[27] So long as the consequent rise in *P'* outstrips the rise in *P*, investment-good output might proceed via forced inflation. But this comes only at the expense of consumer-good output, *R*, meaning, by the First Fundamental Equation, that eventually consumer price inflation will have to catch up.[28] Initial "profit inflation" thus gives way to "income inflation," as factor incomes are bid up by competition between the two sectors, eventually choking off any windfall profits.[29]

Ultimately, as Leijonhufvud notes, "The disequilibrium strain in the economy is brought home on those responsible—*and* in such a way as to induce them to revise that price which is 'wrong' in the 'right' direction."[30] Those speculating against the new natural rate are in essence speculating *against* the price mechanism at work in the fundamental equations. In other words, so long as investment and saving remain out of gear, consequent differentials in relative price levels will exert inexorable equilibrating pressure. The result is that a change in the money supply ultimately alters all prices proportionately.[31]

Where the Wicksell connection asserts itself, therefore, is in the causal role played by the misalignment of market and natural rates of interest and, consequently, saving and investment. Keynes acknowledges the link explicitly, noting that on the question of interest and changes in money prices, "there remains, however, one outstanding attempt at a systematic treatment, namely Knut Wicksell"s *Geldzins und Güterpreise*, published in German in 1898, a book which deserves more fame and much more attention than it has received from English-speaking economists. In substance and intention Wicksell's theory is closely akin...to the theory of this *Treatise*."[32] More specifically, "following Wicksell, it will be convenient to call the rate of interest which would cause the second term of our Fundamental Equation to be zero, the *natural-rate* of interest, and the rate which actually prevails the *market-rate* of interest."[33] He elaborates further, noting that Wicksell's conception of a "natural rate" as the "rate as would obtain if in a non-monetary economy all lending was in the form of actual materials" is in fact "in close accordance with the Fundamental Equation of this Treatise."[34] The reason is that his natural rate, like Wicksell's, constitutes that rate that will be "neutral" with respect to prices, "tending neither to raise nor to lower them." He differs from Wicksell, however, in supposing that a divergence of the money rate from this natural one cannot be indefinitely "cumulative"; such a result must assume that the effect on relative prices does not eventually alter "the mind of the speculator."[35] Equilibrium, or the coincidence of market and natural rates, will be restored, either because speculators who forecast in error are forced to revise their expectations or else because bulls and bears are perfectly balanced.

The Wicksellian influence also manifests itself, however, in the inability of Keynes's model to adequately account for output reactions; à la Wicksell, prices are the sine qua non of the Keynesian cumulative process. In the words of Joan Robinson, we must, therefore, "visualize an acute slump with full employment, and a trade boom without any increase in output."[36,37] To be sure, Keynes did surmise that changes in nominal output would translate, in the short run, into both output and price adjustments. The emergence of windfall losses and the consequent downward pressure on both

P and *P'* will, in the absence of perfect price flexibility, require a fall in *O*. The result must be a "diminution of the volume of employment" of the factors of production *"at the existing rate of earnings,"* such that a "state of unemployment may be expected to ensue, and to continue, until the rise in bank rate is reversed, or by a chance, something happens to alter the natural-rate of interest so as to bring it back to equality with the new market-rate."[38] But *if only* nominal factor earnings could be reduced simultaneously and in equal proportion, "No one need suffer."[39] Keynes's innovation over Wicksell, then, was to explain how changes in relative prices, through the indirect mechanism of entrepreneurial profits, will ultimately redound in a re-equilibrating manner upon the imperfect coordination of market and natural rates of interest.

2.2. *PRICES AND PRODUCTION*

Like Keynes's fundamental equations, Hayek's model in *Prices and Production* rests upon an essential distinction between the separate decisions to save and invest. Hayek, akin to Wicksell and Keynes, notes that "only in comparatively few cases will the people who have saved money and the people who want to use it in production be identical." Rather, "In the majority of cases...the money which is directed to new uses will first have to pass into other hands," namely, the banks. Equilibrium, therefore, will obtain only if the banks, in their lending policy, do not alter the price margins that would have to prevail among various types of capital goods—and, particularly, the equality of these margins with a uniform "natural" rate—in order that consumer output is forthcoming at a rate consistent with consumer demand.[40]

Wicksell's superimposition of the market rate of interest onto the natural, or equilibrium, rate of interest is thus hoisted front and center in Hayek's schema, with Hayek explicitly attributing to Wicksell his conclusion that "so long as the money rate of interest coincides with the equilibrium rate, the rate of interest remains 'neutral' in its effects on the prices of goods, tending neither to raise nor to lower them."[41] For Hayek, the sine qua non of the business cycle is thus the emergence, on account of the intervening influence of money on the rate of interest, of a *dis*proportionality among the various forms of output and, in particular, the excessive production of capital goods.[42]

Keynes's fundamental equations, analogously, turn on the relative prices of consumption and investment goods. But whereas Keynes retains a bare-bones two-sector model, Hayek opts for further disaggregation, constructing a "goods in process" model in which original means of production are successively applied over multiple "stages of production" to eventually yield final, consumable output.[43] The entire "structure of production" is thus interdependent, with the output of any one stage of production dependent upon the output of intermediate goods in all preceding stages. Hayek illustrates this construct in the form of a triangle, as shown in figure 2.2.1.[44] With original factors and other "non-specific producers' goods"[45] applied continuously, the value of intermediate goods forthcoming at a given point in the structure of production is a function of time, $f(t)$, meaning the total value of intermediate products for a production process is $\int_{\tau}^{0} f(t)dt$, where $[\tau, 0]$ is the period of production, and the output of consumers' goods equivalent to $f(0)$.[46,47]

In equilibrium, the distribution of producers' goods across all stages of production will evidently have to be such that no advantage may be attained by shifting resources from one stage to another. For, "It is clear," Hayek writes, "that producers' goods of the same kind which are used in different stages of production cannot, for any length of time, bring in different returns or obtain different

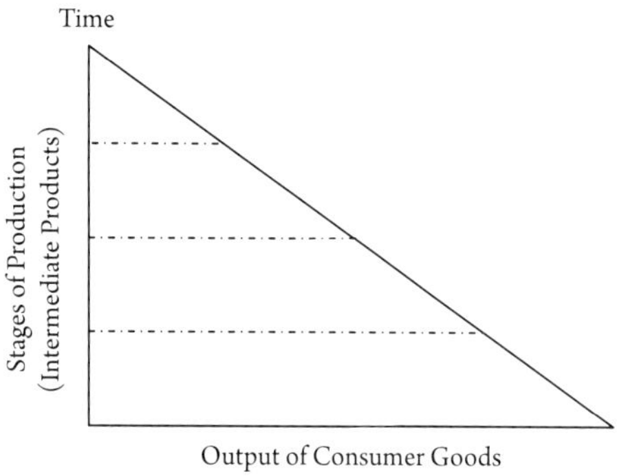

Figure 2.2.1

prices in these different stages."[48] In other words, the delta between the price obtained for the product of any particular stage of production and the prices paid for original means of production and the intermediate products of preceding stages must, in equilibrium, coincide with a uniform rate of profit.[49] Otherwise, the possibility of earning higher returns on producers' goods of a nonspecific sort by investing them in one stage over another will yield a definite arbitrage opportunity.

This element of arbitrage, however, is in fact "a very real and important factor in determining the direction of production," for it is temporary differences between the prices offered in the various stages of production for nonspecific producers' goods that constitute "the *only* means of bringing about a shift of producers' goods from one stage to another."[50] That is, if such a temporary difference in the price margins of different stages of production were to arise, nonspecific producers' goods would eventually be shifted from less to more profitable stages until, owing to diminishing marginal returns, all arbitrage opportunities were exhausted and returns equalized at a single, uniform rate.[51]

The theoretical kinship with Wicksell (and, for that matter, Keynes) should already be recognizable. From Wicksell, Hayek has retained the time element of capital, and in particular the Böhm-Bawerkian reliance on circulating capital. With Keynes as well, however, Hayek shares a sectoral disambiguation that turns on relative profitability. In the fundamental equations, recall, windfall profits performed the task of calling forth greater investment through their impact on relative price levels. In *Prices and Production,* Hayek has merely disaggregated investment, such that the question is no longer simply the bifurcation of resource distribution between consumption and investment but also the allocation of capital among the various "stages" of investment. Nonetheless, the notion of a normal rate of profit at which there is no incentive to shift toward or away from a greater production of consumption goods is fundamental to both models, as well as Wicksell's.

Enter, then, Wicksell's natural rate. Clearly, some margin will have to exist between the cost of inputs and the price of outputs; if not, there exists no incentive to invest. Hayek, following Wicksell, suggests that if saving and investment were to meet in their natural form, as in a nonmonetary barter state, the margin that obtained would be equal to the real rate of return on the capital stock. That is, the uniform price margin established in such a barter state would be identical to the rate of interest, and hence the barter rate is ab ovo the "natural" one.

But Hayek then notes, "I have treated interest as if it were a payment for a definitely given factor of production, like wages or rent," meaning that "in a state of equilibrium these margins are entirely absorbed by interest."[52] Where, however, saving and investment do not meet *in natura,* in the form of real goods, but rather in the form of money, it is then possible that these margins, in real terms, are in fact less or more than entirely absorbed by the rate of interest on money. In other words, it is possible for the money rate of interest to depart from the natural rate (or, indeed, vice versa), with corresponding effects on the price margins prevailing at each stage of production.

Hayek thus considers the case of a fall in the money rate of interest relative to the natural rate, following an expansion of credit by the banking system. "The fall in the rate will," he argues, echoing Wicksell and Keynes, "give a relative advantage to those concerns which use proportionately more capital," or, in Austrian terms, to "longer processes" that can now be capitalized at a lower rate.[53] These more capital-intensive concerns will consequently now be in a position to bid up prices of nonspecific producers' goods, meaning even less capital-intensive firms "will now find it profitable to spend a part of what they previously spent on original means of production, on intermediate products produced by earlier stages of production," and in this way "release" some of the nonspecific goods they previously employed.[54] In other words, the increased cost of producers' goods of a nonspecific type will make it relatively more profitable for producers in all stages to replace these goods with intermediate products, thereby releasing nonspecific producers' goods for investment in longer-term capital projects.[55] Hayek thus posits a "lengthening" of Böhm-Bawerk's average period of production.[56]

Hayek stresses, however, that the switch to more "capitalistic" production processes must be made at the expense of consumption. As producers' goods are invested in projects requiring longer gestation, there will inevitably emerge a shortage in the flow supply of consumer goods relative to demand. "Had saving preceded the change to methods of production of longer duration," Hayek argues, "a reserve of consumers' goods would have been accumulated in the form of increased stocks, which could now be sold at unreduced prices," and thereby serve to bridge the time interval between the moment at which the final products of the original, shorter processes come on to the market, and that at which the first products of the new, longer processes materialize."[57] Instead, the diversion of producers' goods into processes requiring longer gestation will reduce the flow of finished consumer goods, and do so at the same time that the lower money rate of interest discourages saving. The result is a relentless upward pressure on the price of consumer goods, exacerbated by the fact that rising factor incomes in earlier stages of production will almost certainly, assuming no change in consumer preferences, and after only brief time lags, pass through to increased consumer demand.

The mechanism at work is the same as that employed by Wicksell and Keynes: forced saving. Once again, the *sequence* of price effects essentially "forces" real savings into investment via inflation. In Hayek's description, consumers "are forced to forego part of what they used to consume... not because they want to consume less, but because they get less goods for their money income." Thus, there should be no reason to expect that, should money incomes rise again, consumers would not then "immediately attempt to expand consumption to the usual proportion."[58] As in Keynes's fundamental equations, unless new money is forthcoming at an accelerating rate, increased consumer demand must, in conditions of full employment, "*mean a new and reversed change of the proportion between the demand for consumers' goods and the demand for producers' goods in favour of the former.*"[59]

Specifically, the inevitable rise in consumers' goods prices will raise margins in later stages of production, allowing those stages nearest to final consumption to outbid earlier stages for original factors and nonspecific producers' goods.[60] As prices of producers' goods of a nonspecific type are thus bid up, price margins will narrow, but narrow especially in earlier stages.[61] Moreover, producers' goods of a specific nature will tend to fall in price, as they become relatively abundant by reason of the shift to more direct means of production, thereby further squeezing price margins on the production of intermediate goods. "Very soon," Hayek concludes, "the relative rise of the prices of the original factors and the more mobile intermediate products will make the longer processes unprofitable," meaning investment projects undertaken on account solely of loose credit will be rendered untenable and have to be either scaled back or abandoned altogether.[62]

Crucially for Hayek, this retrenchment of longer-term investment, corresponding to a shortening of the average period of production, will transpire even with fixed capital. Unlike Wicksell—who, recall, posited that fixed capital of exceptionally long duration essentially mimics rent-earning factors—Hayek contended that "durable means of production do not represent all the capital that is needed for an increase of output," but rather that in order for fixed capital to be mobilized to full capacity, it is typically necessary "to invest a great amount of other means of production in lengthy processes," in collaboration with those durable goods.[63] In other words, even though capital of exceptional durability may remain physically intact, its full employment nonetheless require the continuous investment of *other* producers' goods in sufficient quantities; producers' goods that, given the rise in consumer demand, are simply not forthcoming.[64]

Hence, the existence of vast stocks of unused capacity, Hayek contends, by no means constitutes proof that the problem is excess capital and insufficient consumption. On the contrary, it is symptomatic of an inability "to use the fixed plant to the full extent because the current demand for consumer goods is too urgent to permit us to invest current productive services in the long processes for which (in consequence of 'misdirections of capital') the necessary durable equipment is available."[65] The scale and composition of investment, therefore, depend not only upon the relative prices of consumer goods and intermediate goods, including fixed capital, but also, and perhaps more saliently, upon the relative prices of nonspecific producers' goods and producers' goods of a more specific sort. This, Hayek concludes, is why it may come about at times that existing resources cannot be fully employed, and how, in such circumstances, it may become impossible to sell them at all, or to sell them only at great loss.[66,67]

Note, however, that as in the Wicksellian and Keynesian accounts, *if only* the money rate of interest tracked the natural rate, there would be no distortion in the structure of production. A successful transition to more (or less) capitalistic methods of production will, unless otherwise impeded by the action of banks, occur if the total demand for consumers' goods (expressed in money) decreases (or increases) relative to the demand for producers' goods.[68] In contrast to inflation-induced forced saving, a voluntary increase in the rate of saving on the part of consumers will, in Hayek's model, imply a narrowing of price margins in later stages of production. Longer investment projects that would previously have been unable to compete with later stages for nonspecific producers' goods will be newly tenable. Likewise, other intermediate stages will be capable of absorbing higher input costs on account of reduced competition for nonspecific producers' goods from later stages of production. Price margins across the entire structure of production will thus, *unless* monetary authorities fail to perceive the shift and persist in maintaining the money rate at its *old* level, narrow, corresponding to a new, lower natural rate.

2.3. THE WICKSELL CONNECTION

Let us recapitulate briefly the manifestation of the Wicksellian theme in its first Keynesian and Hayekian iterations. The money–natural rate distinction is, of course, unmistakable. So too is the potential divergence of investment from saving, which, in both Keynes's fundamental equations and Hayek's triangle, disrupts the equilibrium level of profits and thereby initiates a temporarily cumulative shift toward greater capital intensity. As Keynes puts it:

> The effect of easier credit on the costs of production should be, not to stimulate production all round, but to cause a changeover

> from certain forms of production to other forms; namely, from those for which interest is a relatively unimportant cost to those for which it is a relatively important cost,—which partly depends on the duration of the process of production.[69]

The same point would hardly seem out of place in *Prices and Production*. Indeed, the central thesis of *Prices and Production* is precisely that any conversion from a method of production of some given duration to a method involving more or less time "implies quite definite changes in the organisation of production," and that these changes—functions of the price margins prevailing at each stage of production or, which is the same thing, the rate of interest—will exert a quite definite influence upon "the direction given to the existing productive forces."[70,71] On this point the two theorists were thus of considerable accord.

The first Keynesian and Hayekian iterations of the Wicksellian cumulative process are thus as follows. A lower money rate of interest raises the value of capital projects and thereby allows producers of capital goods to bid factors of production away from processes more directly oriented toward consumption. This is essentially no different from Wicksell's original account. However, the natural rate, and thus saving-consumption preferences, being unchanged,[72] the increased competition from investment for fully employed factors of production will, sooner or later, pass through to higher factor earnings, which will in turn realign relative prices in favor of consumption. So long as the money rate remains pegged below the natural rate, saving and investment will remain out of gear, and the structure of production out of equilibrium, thereby exerting unremitting re-equilibrating pressure on relative prices. All the Wicksellian ingredients are thus in play, but with particular attention to the role of relative prices in arresting the cumulative process.

As Hayek remarks of his own model, however, "To investigate the relationship of these margins to the peculiar advantages of the roundabout methods of production would lead us too far into the problems of the general theory of interest." His premonition is eerily reminiscent of Wicksell's. Nonetheless, Hayek insists that "other things remaining the same—these margins must grow smaller as the roundabout processes of production increase in length and *vice versa*."[73] The errant problems with this lemma, alluded to by Wicksell, are taken up in chapter 3.

NOTES

1. I call this the "second" iteration. Obviously, this label disregards the work of other contemporary economists making use of the Wicksellian framework. Mises preceded Hayek as the founder of Austrian business cycle theory. In Sweden, Cassel, Lindahl, Ohlin, and Myrdal were working to combine sequential analysis with Wicksellian monetary theory, while in England Hawtrey and Robertson further developed loanable funds theory. The purpose of this chapter, however, is to focus attention on the Keynesian and Hayekian models.
2. Using his output identity, $\pi O = PR + P'C$, Keynes disaggregates the respective components, such that:

$$PR = E - S$$

where E is total money income and S income saved. We then have:

$$PR = \frac{E(R+C)}{O} - S \qquad \because O = R + C$$

Or, with I' designating the cost of the flow of new capital goods (i.e., income earned from the production of investment goods):

$$PR = \frac{ER}{O} + I' - S \qquad \because I' = \left(\frac{C}{O}\right)E$$

or

$$P = \frac{E}{O} + \frac{I' - S}{R}$$

This is the "First Fundamental Equation."

The same is then true for investment good output, $P'C$. That is:

$$P'C = E - I'$$

$$P'C = \frac{E(R+C)}{O} - I'$$

$$P'C = \frac{EC}{O} + I - I'$$

where I is the market value of current investment-good output ($I = (R/O)E$). Again aggregating total output:

$$\pi O = \frac{ER}{O} + I' - S + \frac{EC}{O} + I - I'$$

or

$$\pi O = E + I - S$$

In terms of the general price level:

$$\pi = \frac{E}{O} + \frac{I - S}{O}$$

This is Keynes's "Second Fundamental Equation." J. M. Keynes, *A Treatise on Money*, vol. 1, *The Pure Theory of Money* (1930; reprint, London: Macmillan, 1953), 133–150.

3. Hayek actually lamented Keynes's seeming lack of method in his choice of symbols, which "makes it particularly difficult to follow his algebra." F. A. Hayek, "Reflections on the Pure Theory of Money of Mr. J. M. Keynes," *Economica* 11 (1931): 283n.
4. Since $I' = (C/O)E$, we then know that $P'C = (EC/O) + I - I'$, which simplifies to: $(EC/O) + I - (C/O)E = I$.
5. This is an awkward result, but follows from Keynes's (odd) choice to treat the maintenance of existing capital as consumption, whereas only new additions to the capital stock are categorized as "investment." Hayek strongly criticized this method in his review of *A Treatise*. See Hayek, "Reflections on the Pure Theory of Money," 278.
6. Allan H. Meltzer, *Keynes's Monetary Theory* (Cambridge: Cambridge University Press, 1988), 64.
7. Keynes, *A Treatise*, 140.

8. Alternatively, if we take equation 2.1.1, $\pi O = PR + I$, and substitute equations 2.1.2, $\pi O = E + Q$, and (2.1.3), $E = PR + S$, we get $E + Q = E - S + I$. Simplifying, $Q = I - S$. We can also derive this result from the Second Fundamental Equation and equation 2.1.2.
9. Keynes, *A Treatise*, 154–155, 203–206.
10. Ibid.
11. From equation 2.1.3 above. Since Keynes takes output as given, a rise in saving will translate into a fall in the price level, P, of consumption goods.
12. Note that this will be true for both real investment goods and financial assets, since in the case of the latter prices and interest rates move inversely.
13. It should be noted that the sequence here is crucial. If the rise in Q_2 in any way lags the fall in Q_1, aggregate profits may temporarily emerge. But this is of course equivalent to positing a sticky market rate of interest.
14. Keynes, *A Treatise*, 154, 202.
15. Ibid.
16. Ibid., 206, 200–209 (emphasis in original).
17. Though Keynes's primary concern in *A Treatise* was a deflationary Wicksellian cumulative process, we here consider an inflationary case, so as to more readily compare Keynes's model with Wicksell's and Hayek's.
18. In terms of the fundamental equations, this corresponds to a rise in $P'C$ at all interest rates.
19. For the reverse of this scenario, see Axel Leijonhufvud, "The Wicksell Connection: Variations on a Theme," in *Information and Coordination: Essays in Macroeconomic Theory* (New York: Oxford University Press, 1981), 161–162.
20. That is, though $Q = 0$, it may still be true that $Q_1 < 0$ and $Q_2 > 0$, in which case the relative price differential between consumption goods and investment goods will lead to continuous changes in I' (I' must rise) and/or R (R must fall) until price levels are again consistent with zero windfall profits or losses.
21. Essentially, the value of new investment relative to its cost of production will rise and fall on the basis of financiers' appetite for securities versus cash deposits.
22. Keynes, *A Treatise*, 262–275. See also Leijonhufvud, "The Wicksell Connection," 161–162.
23. Leijonhufvud, "The Wicksell Connection," 161–162.
24. Ibid.
25. Keynes, *A Treatise*, 1:262–275.
26. Ibid., 267–269.
27. Thus, $Q_1 = I' - S > 0$, $Q_2 = I - I' > 0$, and $Q = I - S > 0$.
28. Keynes, *A Treatise*, 1:263, 265, 269, 271. We know also that, since $I = (R/O)E$, a fall in R relative to total output will tend to lower the value of investment goods, and thus lower Q_2.
29. That is, in the event of aggregate profits, investment- and consumer-goods producers "bid against one another for the services of the factors of

production, until the latter have risen to a level at which costs of production and sale proceeds are again equal." Keynes, *A Treatise*, 269.

30. Leijonhufvud, "The Wicksell Connection," 164.
31. Keynes, *A Treatise*, 269–270.
32. Ibid., 186.
33. Ibid., 154–155, 196–199. Recalling that the second term in the Second Fundamental Equation is $((I - S)/O)$, the natural rate is thus that rate which will maintain the equivalence of S and I and preserve price level stability ($\Delta\pi = 0$).
34. Ibid., 197.
35. Ibid., 196–198.
36. J. V. Robinson, "A Parable on Savings and Investment," *Economica* 39 (1933): 84.
37. *A Treatise* does include numerous discussions of why, in the real world, changes in nominal income might involve changes in both output and prices. In response to Joan Robinson's 1931 article on this issue, Keynes wrote: "I think you are a little hard on me as regards the assumption of constant output.... I have long discussions [on] the effects of changes in output; it is only at a particular point in the preliminary theoretical argument that I have assumed constant output." Quoted in Robert Skidelsky, *John Maynard Keynes*, vol. 2, *The Economist as Savior 1920–1937* (London: Macmillan, 1983), 448.
38. Keynes, *A Treatise*, 206–207, 263, 269–271 (emphasis added).
39. Ibid., 271. As Leijonhufvud observes, "Output reactions could not be handled by Wicksellians—whether Swedish, British, or Austrian—as of 1930." Leijonhufvud, "The Wicksell Connection," 162–163.
40. F. A. Hayek, *Prices and Production* (London: Routledge, 1931; reprint, New York: Augustus M. Kelley, 1967), 46, 84.
41. Ibid., 24.
42. F. A. Hayek, *Monetary Theory and the Trade Cycle*, trans. N. Kaldor (1929; reprint, London: Harcourt, Brace, 1933), 54 (emphasis in original).
43. Hayek, *Prices and Production*, 40.
44. Hayek attributes his triangle to William Stanley Jevons and Wicksell's *Lectures*. Hayek, *Prices and Production*, 38n. See also Knut Wicksell, *Lectures on Political Economy*, vol. 1, *General Theory*, ed. Lionel Robbins, trans. E. Classen (1901; reprint, London: Routledge & Kegan Paul, 1935), 151–154; William Stanley Jevons, *Theory of Political Economy*, ed. R. D. C. Collison Black (1871; reprint, Baltimore: Penguin Books, 1970), 231.
45. Hayek defines "non-specific producers' goods" as "not only almost all original means of production, but also most raw materials and even a great many implements of a not very specialised kind—knives, hammers, tongs, and so on," noting that this category "will, in particular, comprise most of the goods which at one and the same time belong to different stages." Hayek, *Prices and Production*, 71.
46. The output of consumption goods, $f(0)$, is thus the horizontal leg of Hayek's triangle, the production function, $f(t)$, the hypotenuse, and the integral of $f(t)$ over the entire period of production the area. Ibid., 41n, 41–43.

47. Ibid. It should be noted that the figure represents values rather than physical production.
48. Ibid., 72.
49. Ibid., 49.
50. Ibid., 72 (emphasis added).
51. Ibid.
52. Ibid., 73–74.
53. Ibid., 86.
54. Hayek explains that firms "will, e.g., buy parts of their products, which they used to manufacture themselves, from another firm, and can now employ the labour thus dismissed in order to produce these parts on a large scale with the help of new machinery." Consequently, "those original means of production and non-specific producers' goods which are required in the new stages of production are set free by the transition of the old concerns to more capitalistic methods which is caused by the increase in the prices of these goods." Ibid., 87.
55. It is helpful to visualize this dynamic in terms of Hayek's triangle. Consider a production process, of the flow-input—point-output variety employed by Hayek, in which a single input, a, is applied continuously from time τ to time 0, yielding final consumable output at time 0. Given the rate of interest, r, the value of this investment process can be expressed as:

$$\begin{aligned} V &= \int_{\tau}^{0} a e^{rt} dt \\ &= \frac{-a\left(e^{r\tau}-1\right)}{r} \end{aligned} \tag{2.2.1n}$$

Differentiating with respect to the rate of interest, we have:

$$\frac{\partial V}{\partial r} = \frac{a\left(-r\tau e^{r\tau} + e^{r\tau} - 1\right)}{r^2}$$

which is unambiguously negative for all values of r. In other words, a rise (fall) in the interest rate will, for a flow-input—point-output process, lower (raise) the present discounted value of all investment projects. Moreover, if we take the second derivative with respect to τ, the period of investment, we obtain:

$$\frac{\partial^2 V}{\partial r \partial \tau} = -a\tau e^{r\tau}$$

which is unambiguously positive for all values of r and all $\tau < 0$ (remember that cost-of-input capital valuations are backward-looking), meaning changes in the rate of interest will have *larger* effect on capital values the *longer* is the period of production.

56. With compound interest, the aggregate sum of investment periods is:

$$\sum_{t=0}^{\tau} -a(1+r)^{t}$$
$$= -a\tau(1+r)^{\theta}$$
$$\approx -a\tau e^{r\theta}$$

where θ is the average period of production. Using equation 2.2.1, we can then solve for the average period of production:

$$\frac{a\left(e^{r\theta}-1\right)}{r} = -a\tau e^{r\theta}$$
$$\theta = \frac{-\ln\left(\frac{-1}{r\tau-1}\right)}{r}$$

Differentiating with respect to *r*, we have:

$$\frac{\partial\theta}{\partial r} = \frac{\ln(-1/r\tau-1)}{r^{2}} - \frac{\tau}{r(r\tau-1)}$$

which, for all $\tau < 0$, is unambiguously negative. In other words, a rise (fall) in the rate of interest will shorten (lengthen) the average period of production, as per Hayek's hypothesis.

Hayek's propositions thus seem to be confirmed. However, the reader will note that Hayek's model is of the flow-input—point-output type, with compound interest. As Wicksell observed, and as we can clearly see in the equations above, this means that the value of capital is not independent of the rate of interest. Since capital intensity is, as we saw in chapter 1 with Wicksell effects, affected by the distribution of inputs over the period of production, this dependence will not, in general, be benign. It only appears benign in this example because our model, like Hayek's triangle, assumes one input applied uniformly over time. As we will see in subsequent chapters, more generalized models disrupt the simple parables illustrated above.

57. Hayek, *Prices and Production*, 88.
58. Ibid., 57.
59. Ibid., 89–90 (emphasis in original).
60. Ibid., 91.

61. We can confirm this by finding the cross-derivative of *V* with respect to *a* and τ. We get:

$$\frac{\partial^2 V}{\partial a \partial \tau} = -e^{r\tau}$$

which is unambiguously negative for all $\tau < 0$, meaning rising input prices will tend to raise values of shorter investment processes by proportionately more than longer processes.
62. Ibid., 92.
63. Ibid., 95–96.
64. "The situation would be similar," Hayek suggests, "to that of a people of an isolated island if, after having partially constructed an enormous machine which was to provide them with all the necessities, they found out that they had exhausted all their savings and available free capital before the new machine could turn out its product." They would then "have no choice but to abandon temporarily the work on the new process and to devote all their labour to producing their daily food without any capital." Ibid., 94.
65. Ibid., 96
66. Ibid.
67. There is an asymmetry, acknowledged by Hayek, between the transition to longer processes of production and the transition back to shorter ones, with the former proceeding without unemployment, and the latter being often accompanied by crisis. Hayek attributes this asymmetry to the fact that "in the former case there will necessarily be time to amortize the capital invested in the existing structure before the new process is completed, while in the latter case this will evidently be impossible and therefore a loss of capital and a reduction of income inevitable." Ibid., 93n.
68. Hayek, *Prices and Production*, 50.
69. Keynes, *A Treatise*, 211.
70. Hayek, *Prices and Production*, 35, 38.
71. Both Keynes and Hayek contend that the primary consequence of interest is not its role as a cost factor but rather its effect on prices. Hayek contends that "to think of interest only as a direct cost factor is to overlook its main influence on production. What is much more important is its effect on prices through its effect on demand for the intermediate products and for the factors from which they are produced." Ibid., 83. Similarly, Keynes argues that "a fall in the rate of interest stimulates the production of capital-goods not because it decreases their cost of production but because it increases their demand price." Keynes, *A Treatise*, 211.
72. Or even distorted, on account of the lower money rate of interest, toward a *greater* preference for present consumption.
73. Hayek, *Prices and Production*, 74.

Chapter 3

The Sraffa Connection

In light of the theoretical antagonism later associated with the Keynes-Hayek controversies, pedantry about the degree to which Keynes and Hayek were in fact in considerable accord in *A Treatise* and *Prices and Production* is well worth the while. Here, the Wicksell connection is crucial. In both iterations of the Wicksellian theme, the business cycle is rooted in an unresolved conflict within the structure of production, between consumption goods and investment goods, which is strictly correlated with the failure of adjustment between saving and investment. The potential divergence between the money and Wicksellian natural rates of interest constitutes a monetary trip wire within the price system. While both concede, in line with Wicksell, that forced saving may temporarily divert original factors from the production of consumer into the production of capital goods, ultimately the real resource constraint of full employment is decisive; rising factor-price inflation arrests the cumulative process.

It is thus that when Hayek, at Lionel Robbins's urging, unleashed an exacting, fifty-six-page review of what Keynes had hoped would be his magnum opus in the August 1931 issue of *Economica*, it was not without praise. "The new approach, which Mr. Keynes has adopted," he wrote, "which makes the rate of interest and its relation to saving and investing the central problem of monetary theory, is an enormous advance."[1] He furthermore noted that "it is even possible that in the end it will turn out that there exists less difference between

Mr. Keynes's views and my own than I am at present inclined to assume."[2] Nonetheless, Hayek's review spared little mercy, and the ensuing tripartite exchange among Hayek, Keynes, and Sraffa—highly abstract, often impenetrably abstruse, and occasionally acerbic—revealed that the unresolved capital-theoretic puzzles in the Wicksellian framework, particularly the complications posed by Wicksell effects, lingered in both the Keynesian and Hayekian models.

Here, we distill each of the three positions in turn, beginning with Hayek's review of *A Treatise* and Keynes's response, and concluding with Sraffa's excoriating assessment of *Prices and Production*. Beneath the sharp rhetoric and terminological farrago of the battling reviews, we will see that just as Hayek and Keynes shared the positive elements of the Wicksell connection—the money–natural rate distinction and the saving-investment mechanism—so too did they share its theoretical albatross, namely, the problem of addressing how changes in relative prices will redound upon the value of capital. Moreover, Sraffa's review would compound the challenge by observing that in a multicommodity world, there is no single rate that will obviously recommend itself as *the* natural rate. Any further development of the Wicksell connection by Keynes and Hayek would, therefore, have to remedy these deficiencies.

3.1. HAYEK ON KEYNES

The primary target of Hayek's review is Keynes's failure, in Hayek's view, "to realise the necessity of dealing with the all-important problem of changes in the value of existing capital," a failure that, according to Hayek, "is also partly responsible for the deficiencies of [Keynes's] concept of capital."[3] The terminological miasma that engulfs the Hayek-Keynes debate has tended to obscure this fundamental point.[4]

Recall from Keynes's fundamental equations that a fall in the money rate will, if unaccompanied by a corresponding fall in the natural rate, raise P', thereby stimulating increased production of investment goods and inducing a decline in the supply of household savings. As windfall profits consequently emerge in the production first of investment goods, then of consumer goods, factor earnings are bid up, such that eventually all prices rise proportionately. And if, on the other hand, the money rate does unerringly track the natural rate, a change in the latter, while giving rise to windfall profits or losses in *either* the consumer-goods *or* investment-goods sector, will not generate windfall profits in the aggregate, meaning the overall price level remains unaffected.[5]

The problem with this story, Hayek contends, is that it assumes a rigid structure of production.[6] Keynes's fundamental equations make no provision for the possibility that inasmuch as the production of investment goods is stimulated by windfall profits, it will likely also involve changes in the rate of efficiency earnings, (E/O), which Keynes's analysis assumes to be fixed. His putative equation of the natural rate with the rate that will secure aggregate price-level stability ignores the fact that efficiency earnings will actually "change with every change of the price of the units of the factors of production (including interest) as well as with every change in the organisation of production."[7,8] In other words, every increment of capital investment will involve not only changes in the average price of the factors of production but also changes in their relative prices, which will, in general, induce changes in production technique and, consequently, in the amount of output produced by a given quantity of factors of production.[9]

This critique should be immediately recognizable from chapter 1. It was, after all, Wicksell who realized that "it is futile to attempt...to derive the value of capital-goods from their own cost of production or reproduction; for in fact these costs of production include *capital* and interest."[10] As Hayek notes, Keynes's simplified identities involve him in "serious difficulties," in that he fails to specify whether any increase in the *value* of *existing* capital is to be counted as additional capital, without the production of any new capital goods, or else whether only additions to the *physical* stock of capital goods comprise new investment.[11] Channeling Wicksell, Hayek further emphasizes that this latter approach "becomes clearly impossible when the old capital goods are not replaced by goods of exactly the same kind," but instead constitute a transition to more capitalistic methods of production, whereby capital goods of a prior vintage are replaced by those of a newer variety. Wicksell effects strike back.

Accordingly, Hayek seals his critique by referring back to the theoretical foundation upon which Keynes's *Treatise* was explicitly premised, namely, Wicksell. Of the capital-theoretic shortcomings in *A Treatise*, Hayek suggests that while "Mr. Keynes tries to incorporate into his system the ideas of Wicksell," he neglects the fact that "in Wicksell's system these are necessary outgrowths of the most elaborate theory of capital we possess, that of Böhm-Bawerk." Thus, noting that "it is a priori unlikely that an attempt to utilise the conclusions drawn from a certain theory without accepting that theory itself should be successful," Hayek drives home his point by insisting that "Mr. Keynes ignores completely the general theoretical basis of Wicksell's theory."[12] Keynes's Wicksell connection, in other words, was short-circuited.

3.2. KEYNES ON HAYEK

Keynes peppered his copy of Hayek's twenty-six-page review with thirty-four pencil marks, scribbling, on the last page, that "Hayek has not read my book with that measure of 'good will' which an author is entitled to expect of a reader."[13] His reply, appearing in *Economica* before the second half of Hayek's review even reached print, was less resigned. Of *Prices and Production*, Keynes declared that "the book, as it stands, seems to me to be one of the most frightful muddles I have ever read, with scarcely a sound proposition in it...an extraordinary example of how, starting with a mistake, a remorseless logician can end up in Bedlam."[14]

Despite contrariwise entangling himself in the terminological labyrinth of this very "Bedlam," Keynes nonetheless, toward the latter half of his reply, confronts the capital-theoretic challenge laid bare in Hayek's review, acknowledging as "the underlying cause" of Hayek's discontent the fact that "I do not myself propound any satisfactory theory of capital and interest and that I do not build on any existing theory." Specifically, he admits to neglecting the task of elucidating the relationship between capital accumulation, and the rate of consumption and the factors determining the natural rate of interest, even going so far as to concede that "I agree with Dr. Hayek that a development of this theory would be highly relevant to my treatment of monetary matters and likely to throw light into dark corners." But while conceding that the essential ideas at which Böhm-Bawerk was driving may, ultimately, be found to lie at the heart of the capital problem, and that neglect of him by prewar English economists "was as mistaken as their neglect of Wicksell," he denies that Böhm-Bawerk's constitutes a satisfactory theory of capital, and furthermore suggests that the pursuit of such theoretical mammon "might lead one rather a long way from monetary theory," with which both he and Hayek were ostensibly concerned.[15]

Keynes thus accedes to the central thrust of Hayek's critique, noting, on the question of Wicksell's capital theory, that "substantially I concede Dr. Hayek's point," and that he agreed that a formal account of the factors determining the natural rate of interest ought to figure prominently in a revised *Treatise*. "I can only plead," he writes, "that I had much to say for which such a theory is not required and that my own ideas about it were still too much in embryo to deserve publication. Later on, I will endeavour to make good this deficiency."[16] It was likewise on this note that Keynes concluded a direct exchange of twelve letters with Hayek regarding the latter's review, closing with the concessionary remark that he doubted if he would "return to the charge," given that he was then attempting to "re-shape and improve my central position," and "that is probably a better way to spend one's time than in controversy."[17]

Keynes, however, by no means granted Hayek a complete Wicksellian pass. For while he confessed that he had not, in *A Treatise*, satisfactorily accounted for the determinants of the natural rate of interest, he also insisted that "a little consideration of [Hayek's] problem...brings out the point that the term 'natural rate of interest' is not altogether free from ambiguity."[18] Keynes's conception of Wicksell's "natural rate" was, he argued, merely that rate which would equalize saving and investment, given the prevailing psychology of the market and including any temporary errors in forecasting, irrespective of whether the corresponding rate of investment was expected to be permanent. Hayek, he contended, was concerned with the more conjectural notion of a "long-period" equilibrium rate absent forecasting errors and consistent with the expectation that the prevailing ratio of capital to consumption is to remain permanent. While this latter conception may, Keynes granted, have something to recommend itself for the analysis of "long-period" shifts of the natural rate, such analysis would involve one in exceedingly complicated capital-theoretic issues, not all of which were strictly required by the concerns of monetary theory.[19]

Keynes's final parting shot, therefore, was to suggest that "Dr. Hayek has seen a vision, and though when he woke up he has made nonsense of his story by giving the wrong names to the objects which occur in it, his Khubla Khan is not without inspiration and must set the reader thinking with the germs of an idea in his head."[20] As we will see in chapter 4, evidently Keynes's exchange with Hayek did "set him thinking."

3.3. SRAFFA ON HAYEK

The substance of Keynes's direct discourse with Hayek in the wake of the *Economica* review—carried out in twelve letters between December 1931 and March 1932—was thus dominated by attempts to make sense of the "names" and "objects" to which both protagonists had attached often impenetrably recondite technical jargon, a task that left Keynes discernibly weary. But the Wicksell connection detained his interest nonetheless. Shortly before his final letter to Hayek regarding *A Treatise*, Keynes sent a terse note to fellow Cantabrigians Piero Sraffa and Richard Kahn, asking, "What is the next move? I feel that the abyss yawns—and so do I. Yet I can't help feeling that there *is* something interesting in it."[21,22] One month later, in what Geoffrey Harcourt would subsequently call the superlative example of an academic "hatchet job," Sraffa, at Keynes's invitation as editor, unleashed a devastating review of *Prices and Production* in Cambridge's *Economic Journal*.[23]

Sraffa's review zeroed in on two cardinal points of Hayek's theory, both of which are intimately related to the Wicksell connection. First, Sraffa questioned why capital accumulated by means of forced saving must ultimately be dissipated once the forced saving ceases. Second, he challenged the very notion of "*the*" natural rate of interest. The former point constituted the brunt of Sraffa's opening salvo. The problem, he contended, was that the sine qua non of Hayek's theory, namely, the supposed inadequacy of "involuntary" capital accumulation, was not borne out by his theory. Hayek, recall, had claimed that in the case of forced saving, the sacrifice of current consumption "is not made by those who will reap the benefit from the new investments."[24] Consequently, he had concluded, "There can be no doubt" that once factor incomes rise, consumers will "immediately attempt to expand consumption to the usual proportion," and there will be an inevitable retrenchment in capital investment as previously invested capital is, in essence, consumed.

Yet to this proposition Sraffa counters:

> As a moment's reflection will show, "there can be no doubt" that nothing of the sort will happen. One class has, for a time, robbed another class of part of their incomes; and has saved the plunder. When the robbery comes to an end, it is clear that the victims cannot possibly consume the capital which is now well out of their reach.[25]

His objection should be familiar from Wicksell's original account of the cumulative process; in essence, Sraffa has merely repackaged Wicksell's notion of capital maturation in explicitly classist form. The crucial point is that Sraffa sees no reason to assume that capital projects undertaken by means of forced saving will be incapable of completion before forced saving is choked off, and claims that "Dr. Hayek fails to prove the contrary."[26] He reinforces this point by noting that if only credits were apportioned among producers and consumers so as not to disturb initial proportions, there would be no forced saving. And if, in the event of forced saving, banks were to increase the quantity of producer credits to the same extent that they decreased the quantity of consumer credits, there would be no crisis. Thus Sraffa concludes that "an extraneous element, in the shape of the supposed power of the banks to settle the way in which money is spent, has crept into the argument and has done all the work."[27]

But here Sraffa seems to have been mistaken. For Hayek was *not* arguing, as Sraffa suggests he was, that credit expansion must assume the form of increased availability of credit to producers over consumers, but rather simply that looser credit, as manifested in a lower money rate of interest, will be particularly favorable to investment of an exceptionally long duration. This much should have been clear to any student of Wicksell. In other words, earlier stages of production are initially able to outbid later stages for producers' goods not because credits are granted to them, and not to later stages, but rather because a lower rate of discount disproportionately raises the value of lengthy investment projects, such that producers in earlier stages are now willing and able to bid more, relative to producers in later stages, for original means and other nonspecific producers' goods.[28]

Sraffa, therefore, is entirely correct to observe that *if only* the banks were to somehow apportion credit evenly among producers and consumers, then there would, indeed, be no inducement to change within the time structure of production. But, as Hayek countered, Sraffa's approach is merely to "ignore the fact that an expansion of credit via the Bank Rate mechanism will not 'apportion the additional money between consumers and producers so as not to disturb the initial proportions,' but will certainly favour the 'higher' stages at the expense of the 'lower,'" not due to any contrivance by the banks, but rather to the operation of the interest rate on relative prices.[29] In other words, money (as Wicksell was keen to demonstrate), is *never* evenly apportioned, in the sense that to each dollar in possession another is added, which means the greater or less of it will always differentially impact the present value of capital projects of varying durations.

As for Sraffa's charge that "there can be no doubt" capital accumulated by means of forced saving is no less permanent than capital accumulated via voluntary saving, Hayek appealed, implicitly, to price Wicksell effects, noting that "if entrepreneurs in one stage of production find it impossible or unprofitable to replace e.g. their machines, then this will cause the capital instruments which are devoted to the production of these machines to lose their value." Moreover, "That the physical quantity of these capital goods will, for some time, continue to exist unchanged does not mean that their owners have not lost the greater part, or all, of their capital." Here, indeed, is the very definition of the price Wicksell effect, with Hayek further adding that "it is of very little use for the machine manufacturer to hold on tight to his capital goods when the producer who used to buy the machines is either unable, or finds it unprofitable at the higher rate of interest, to do so now. Whether he likes it or not, the actions of other people have destroyed his capital."[30] In essence, Hayek is suggesting that the relative price changes triggered by monetary disturbances will induce both price and real Wicksell effects, initially as forces of disequilibration, later as re-equilibrating ones—the "complications" to which Wicksell referred.

Nonetheless, Sraffa's "surprisingly superficial objection" in fact posed a more profound challenge than Hayek (and perhaps, for that matter, Sraffa) perceived.[31] The problem is that Wicksell effects cut both ways; the circular dependence of the value of capital on the rate of interest and vice versa means that in a world of heterogeneous capital, there is simply no well-behaved, inverse monotonic relationship between capital intensity and the rate of interest. When different inputs are invested in different proportions at various points in time, a change in the relative price of any one of these inputs will alter the average period of production. In other words, the fact that inputs are weighted according not only to the quantity invested but also to the length of time for which they are invested, razes any notion of a unique average period of production. Hayek, armed with Austrian capital theory, thus "builds up a terrific steam-hammer in order to crack a nut—and then he does not crack it."[32] Hayek's theory asserts unambiguously signed price effects as the interest rate varies, but with Wicksell effects, ambiguity is inescapable.

Hence, by forcing Hayek to emphasize the role of capital revaluations, over the "supposed power of the banks" in driving the cycle, Sraffa's critique also hoisted upon Hayek all the theoretical baggage of Wicksell effects, with which Hayek would have to contend. Hayek himself, while acknowledging that it was upon the question of capital consumption that "my theory stands or falls," also insisted that "to describe in detail the process by which the additional capital is consumed would be a lengthy task, which I hope to undertake soon in another place."[33] As Keynes prophetically predicted, this would ultimately lead Hayek some way from monetary theory.[34]

Having exposed the capital-theoretic shortcomings of the Austro-Wicksellian approach, Sraffa next turned his attack to the core of the Wicksell connection, namely, the natural rate of interest. The Wicksellian money–natural rate framework, Sraffa argues, is marked by "an essential confusion . . . which identifies the 'actual' with the 'money' rate, and the 'equilibrium' with the 'natural' rate." For, Sraffa objects, "If money did not exist, and loans were made in terms of all sorts of commodities, there would be a single rate which satisfies the conditions of equilibrium, but there might be at any one moment as many 'natural' rates of interest as there are commodities, though they would not be 'equilibrium' rates."[35] In other words, without money, commodities would necessarily be exchanged directly for themselves or each other, across the same or different time periods, in "natural" form, such that saving and investment would be defined in purely real, physical terms, with the rate of interest referring to the ratio between a physical quantity of a given commodity today and the quantity it trades for at some future date.[36]

A moment's reflection, however, reveals that, in Sraffa's words, "the 'arbitrary' action of the banks," the cornerstone of the Wicksell-

Hayek-Keynes story, is "by no means" a necessary condition for the divergence of the money rate from the natural rate. For "if loans were made in wheat and farmers (or for that matter the weather) 'arbitrarily changed' the quantity of wheat produced, the actual rate of interest on loans in terms of wheat would diverge from the rate on other commodities and there would be no single equilibrium rate."[37] Equilibrium, therefore, refers strictly to a situation in which the spot and future prices of each commodity or capital good coincide, and all of these "natural" or "commodity" rates of interest are equal to one another, and to the money rate. But if, for any reason, supply and demand for a commodity or capital good deviate from their long-period equilibrium position—as will necessarily be the case in an expanding economy—the spot and forward prices of that commodity will diverge, and the "natural" rate of interest on that commodity will depart from the "natural" rates on all other commodities. Thus, it marks an "essential confusion" to speak of a hypothetical barter rate as the "natural" or "equilibrium" rate, since the potential divergence of different rates of interest exists just the same in a barter economy as in a monetary one, and, indeed, "There may be as many 'natural' rates as there are commodities," as well as, for each commodity, different "natural" rates for loans of different lengths.[38]

Sraffa, however, insists that while his argument may constitute a criticism of Hayek, it "is not itself a criticism of Wicksell." "For there is," he argues, "a 'natural' rate of interest which, if adopted as bank-rate, will stabilize a price-level (i.e. the price of a composite commodity): it is an average of the 'natural' rates of the commodities entering into the price-level, weighted in the same way as they are in the price-level itself"—in other words, an aggregate index of barter rates.[39] Where Sraffa does object to Wicksell, however, is on the supposition that such a price level is unique. For any composite commodity arbitrarily selected, Sraffa claims, "There is a corresponding rate that will equalize the purchasing power, in terms of that composite commodity, of the money saved and of the additional money borrowed for investment."[40] That is, because the composite rate is a weighted average of the natural rates entering into it, setting the money rate equal to this composite rate, while inducing relative price changes among the commodities entering into the price level, will nonetheless hold the nominal aggregate price level constant. Hence, the purchasing power of money saved and invested will be stable in terms of the particular composite commodity chosen. This result, however, would obtain for any arbitrarily selected composite commodity.[41]

Hayek's reply was tentative. In response to Sraffa's hypothetical barter economy, Hayek suggested that "it would be truer to say that, in this situation, there would be *no single rate* which, applied to all commodities, would satisfy the conditions of equilibrium rates, but there might, at any moment, be as many 'natural' rates of interest as there are commodities, *all* of which would be *equilibrium rates*."[42] The "natural" rate of interest on a loan of strawberries, for example, from July to January would presumably be negative, while the natural rates on loans of most other commodities over the same period would be positive.[43] To this Sraffa replied with sardonic glee, writing in his rejoinder to Hayek's reply that "Dr. Hayek now acknowledges the multiplicity of the 'natural' rates, but he has nothing more to say on this specific point than that they 'all would be equilibrium rates.' The only meaning (if it be a meaning) I can attach to this is that his maxim of policy now requires that the money rate should be equal to all these divergent natural rates."[44]

Ludwig Lachmann would later call Hayek's admission that there might be no single rate "a fatal concession," asking, like Sraffa, "What, then, becomes of monetary equilibrium?"[45] Sraffa's scathing riposte aside, however, Hayek's statement is not only correct but also constitutes a theoretical escape hatch from the pitfalls of

Wicksellian natural rate theory. For Hayek's proposition does not deny that in a barter economy, commodity arbitrage would tend to produce an overall equilibrium rate of interest; otherwise, if the rate of interest on strawberries were lower than the rate on cotton, there would exist an arbitrage opportunity to borrow in strawberries and lend in cotton. This does not, however, mean that all commodity rates must be equal but rather simply that any disparities between two commodity rates are exactly compensated by disparities in relative forward prices, such that, in terms of any third commodity serving as numéraire, it is no more profitable to lend in cotton than in strawberries. The hypothetical overall equilibrium rate thus obtaining would then be consistent with all the factors "affecting the present and future supply of the individual commodities," simultaneously determined.[46]

It is certainly conceivable, Hayek concedes, for any one of these commodity rates to be out of equilibrium, just as any price may be out of equilibrium. "But the only essential point at issue here," he argues, "is whether the fact that any of these 'natural' rates, in terms of a single commodity, may be out of equilibrium... can have effects which are anything like those of a divergence between the actual money rate and the equilibrium rate which is due to an increase in the quantity of money." In other words, it is the particular properties of money itself that permit artificial distortion of the time structure of production, in a way that other commodity rates will not. "The inter-relation between these different rates of interest," Hayek determined, however, "is far too complicated to allow of detailed discussion within the compass of this reply."[47] Hayek as well, it seems, was looking to "re-shape and improve" his central position. The nagging problem was, once commodity rates and forward prices were at their equilibrium, market-clearing levels, what, exactly, was the "equilibrium" rate to which Hayek referred? Presumably, it would be the difference, after arbitrage, between the price obtained for the product of each particular stage of production and the prices paid for original means of production and the intermediate products of all preceding stages, once all prices have been reconciled to their equilibrium, market-clearing values. But Hayek failed to articulate this point.

What, then, are we to conclude from this protracted, and no doubt abstruse, tripartite exchange? To summarize, we have found that while Keynes's *Treatise* model lacked capital-theoretic foundations, and in particular a satisfactory account of the natural rate of interest, Hayek's capital theory was critically undermined by the complicating factor of Wicksell effects. Moreover, both were impacted by Sraffa's reminder that in a multicommodity world, there may be any number of "natural" rates, and thus it is not even remotely axiomatic which one, of many, should be identified as *the* natural rate. Indeed, Hayek's critique of Keynes's inadequately developed natural rate theory could, in light of Sraffa's review, be turned with some justification back upon himself. The solution to this dilemma for the Wicksell connection, however, was suggested by Sraffa, in the form of some "composite" commodity, the natural rate of which we might define as *the* natural rate. Sraffa's answer, however, raises two fresh challenges, with which Keynes and Hayek would have to contend. First, which composite commodity, out of innumerable possibilities, do we select? Second, how does the corresponding natural rate interact with money? We take up the Keynesian and Hayekian answers to these questions in the next two chapters.

NOTES

1. F. A. Hayek, "Reflections on the Pure Theory of Money of Mr. J. M. Keynes," *Economica* 11 (1931): 270.
2. Ibid., 295.
3. Ibid., 281.

4. For a general overview of the Hayek-Keynes and Hayek-Sraffa exchanges, see Bruce Caldwell, "Introduction," in *The Collected Works of F. A. Hayek*, ed. Bruce Caldwell, vol. 9, *Contra Keynes and Cambridge: Essays and Correspondence* (Chicago: University of Chicago Press, 1995), 21–40; H. D. Kurz, "The Hayek-Keynes-Sraffa Debate Reconsidered," in *Critical Essays on Piero Sraffa's Legacy in Economics*, ed. H. D. Kurz (Cambridge: Cambridge University Press, 2000), 279–283.
5. Recall that $Q_1 = I' - S$ and $Q_2 = I - I'$. Since $P'C = I$, a change in the rate of interest will, by changing P', result in $Q_2 \neq 0$. But because, in this case, the money rate is assumed to track the natural rate, $I = S$, meaning windfall profits or losses in the investment-goods sector will be exactly matched by windfall losses or profits in the consumption-goods sector. Therefore, $Q = Q_1 + Q_2 = I' - S + I - I' = I - S = 0$, and $\pi = ((E/O) = ((I-S)/O) = (E/O))$.
6. Hayek, "Reflections on the Pure Theory of Money" (1931), 273.
7. Acknowledging that Wicksell also supposed that a money rate set equal to the natural rate will secure both the equality of saving and investment *and* price-level stability, Hayek remarks that "this is a point on which, in my view, Wicksell was wrong." F. A. Hayek, "Reflections on the Pure Theory of Money of Mr. J. M. Keynes (continued)," *Economica* 12 (1932): 24.
8. Hayek, "Reflections on the Pure Theory of Money" (1931), 289.
9. Ibid.
10. Knut Wicksell, *Lectures on Political Economy*, vol. 1, *General Theory*, ed. Lionel Robbins, trans. E. Classen (1901; London: George Routledge and Sons, 1935), 149 (emphasis in original).
11. Hayek, "Reflections on the Pure Theory of Money" (1931), 279.
12. Ibid., 279.
13. Quoted in Robert Skidelsky, *John Maynard Keynes*, vol. 2, *The Economist as Savior 1920–1937* (London: Macmillan, 1983), 456–457.
14. J. M. Keynes, "The Pure Theory of Money: A Reply to Dr. Hayek," *Economica* 11 (1931): 394.
15. Ibid.
16. Ibid., 395.
17. J. M. Keynes to F. A. Hayek, March 29, 1932, in *The Collected Works of F. A. Hayek*, 9:173. For all of the Hayek-Keynes correspondence regarding *A Treatise* and *Prices and Production*, see *The Collected Works of F. A. Hayek*, 9:164–173.
18. Keynes, "Pure Theory of Money," 395.
19. Ibid.
20. Ibid., 394. For Hayek's response, see F. A. Hayek, "A Rejoinder to Mr. Keynes," *Economica* 11 (1931): 398–403.
21. J. M. Keynes to Piero Sraffa and R. F. Kahn, February 1, 1932, in *The Collected Works of F. A. Hayek*, 9:172 (emphasis in original).

22. Heinz Kurz suggests that Keynes's lack of familiarity with Continental economics and, indeed, with Wicksell's own contributions to capital theory, limited his ability to respond effectively to Hayek's criticisms. Sraffa, only recently arrived from Italy and well versed in alternative (i.e., non-Cambridge) schools of thought, was thus a natural resource. So too was Kahn, who was soon to undertake the task of translating Wicksell's work into English for the Royal Economic Society. See Kurz, "The Hayek-Keynes-Sraffa Debate," 283.
23. G. C. Harcourt, "Keynes, Joan Robinson and The General Theory" (talk given to the Keynes Seminar at the University of Cambridge, January 28, 2009).
24. F. A. Hayek, *Prices and Production*, 2d ed. (1931; reprint, London: Routledge and Kegan Paul, 1935), 57.
25. Sraffa further adds: "If they are wage-earners, who have all the time consumed every penny of their income, they have no wherewithal to expand consumption. And if they are capitalists, who have not shared in the plunder, they may indeed be induced to consume now a part of their capital by the fall in the rate of interest; but not more so than if the rate had been lowered by the 'voluntary savings' of other people." Piero Sraffa, "Dr. Hayek on Money and Capital," *Economic Journal* 42 (1932): 48.
26. Ibid., 47.
27. Ibid., 49.
28. Though, as we shall later see, with Wicksell effects, this proposition is not generally tenable.
29. F. A. Hayek, "Money and Capital: A Reply," *Economic Journal* 42 (1932): 245.
30. Ibid., 243.
31. Ibid. It is unclear when Sraffa first became aware of the challenge posed by Wicksell effects to Neoclassical capital theory. "Perverse" negative Wicksell effects were certainly clear to him by the time of his 1960 magnum opus, *Production of Commodities by Means of Commodities*. But, according to G. C. Harcourt, as early as 1936 Sraffa had written to Joan Robinson explaining the essence of Wicksell effects, and the complications they posed for Neoclassical theory. See Avi J. Cohen and G. C. Harcourt, "Retrospectives: Whatever Happened to the Cambridge Capital Theory Controversies?," *Journal of Economic Perspectives* 17 (2003): 203; Piero Sraffa, *Production of Commodities by Means of Commodities: Prelude to a Critique of Economic Theory* (Cambridge: Cambridge University Press, 1960).
32. Sraffa further adds, in a covert swipe at Austrian capital theory, that "since we are primarily concerned in this review with the nut that is not cracked, we need not spend time criticising the hammer." Sraffa, "Money and Capital," 45.

33. Hayek, "Money and Capital," 239, 243.
34. One of the direct consequences of the Hayek-Sraffa exchange on capital durability was the protracted debate between Hayek and Frank Knight over Austrian capital theory. Knight does seem to have been motivated by Sraffa's review. Shortly after the review appeared, Knight wrote to Oskar Morgenstern, remarking, "I wish he [Hayek] or someone would try to tell me in a plain grammatical sentence what the controversy between Sraffa and Hayek is about. I haven't been able to find anyone on this side who has the least idea." Frank Knight to Oskar von Morgenstern, December 19, 1932, Oskar Morgenstern Papers, Manuscript Department, William R. Perkins Library, Duke University, Raleigh. Unfortunately, it is beyond the scope of this chapter to explore in detail the protracted capital controversy between Knight and Hayek of 1931–1944. For an analysis of the debate, see Avi J. Cohen, "The Hayek/Knight Capital Controversy: The Irrelevance of Roundaboutness, or Purging Processes in Time?," *History of Political Economy* 35 (2003): 469–490; A. J. Cohen, "Frank Knight's Position on Capital and Interest: Foundation of the Hayek/Knight/Kaldor Debate," in *The Economic Mind in America: Essays in the History of American Economics*, ed. M. Rutherford (London: Routledge, 1998).
35. Sraffa, "Money and Capital," 49.
36. Sraffa further elaborates by noting that "loans are currently made in the present world in terms of every commodity for which there is a forward market." For example, "When a cotton spinner borrows a sum of money for three months and uses the proceeds to purchase spot, a quantity of raw cotton which he simultaneously sells three months forward, he is actually 'borrowing cotton' for that period. The rate of interest which he pays, per hundred bales of cotton, is the number of bales that can be purchased with the following sum of money: the interest on the money required to buy spot 100 bales, plus the excess (or minus the deficiency) of the spot over the forward prices of the 100 bales." Ibid., 49–50.
37. Ibid., 49.
38. Ibid., 50. Indeed, Sraffa's point calls into question Hayek's implicit assumption that a barter economy would be inherently more stable. With a multiplicity of "natural" rates, it is, in fact, conceivable that the barter economy would be *more* prone to fluctuations, since we would have now to deal with many more sources of disturbance. For a more comprehensive explanation of Sraffa's notion of commodity rates of interest and his review of *Prices and Production*, see M. S. Lawlor, *The Economics of Keynes in Historical Context* (New York: Palgrave Macmillan, 2006), 213–243. Also, M. S. Lawlor and B. Horn, "Notes on the Sraffa-Hayek Exchange," *Review of Political Economy* 4 (1992): 317–340.
39. Sraffa, "Money and Capital," 51.

40. Ibid.
41. Sraffa would, of course, later propose just such a composite commodity with his "standard commodity." See Sraffa, *Production of Commodities by Means of Commodities: Prelude to a Critique of Economic Theory.*
42. Hayek, "Money and Capital: A Reply," 245.
43. Ibid.
44. Piero Sraffa, "Money and Capital: A Rejoinder," *Economic Journal* 42 (1932): 251.
45. Ludwig Lachmann, "Austrian Economics under Fire: The Hayek-Sraffa Duel in Retrospect," in *Expectations and the Meaning of Institutions: Essays in Economics*, ed. Don Lavoie (London: Routledge, 1994), 154.
46. Hayek, "Money and Capital: A Reply," 246–247.
47. Ibid., 245–246.

Chapter 4

The General Theory

It is hardly surprising that Leijonhufvud would refer to Keynes's second iteration of the Wicksell connection, *The General Theory,* as an "obfuscation."[1] One in fact need look no further than the frustratingly confusing chapter 17, "Properties of Interest and Money," in which Keynes stakes out his second variation on the Wicksellian theme. Indeed, Alvin Hansen, who not only brought Keynesianism to academic America but also, with Hicks, embalmed Keynes in the neo-Walrasian *IS/LM* model, declared chapter 17 merely "another detour which could be omitted without sacrificing the main argument," thereby concluding that it contains "no gold mines."[2] Echoing Hansen, renowned historian of economics Mark Blaug writes that the "two gnomic chapters 16 and 17 are detours which can be omitted without sacrificing the main argument but which, nevertheless, are deep and profound essays on the properties of capital and money."[3,4] If Keynes's "deep and profound" insights on capital and money are regarded as mere "detours," then the Wicksell connection *should* seem "obfuscated."[5]

The confusion stems in no small part from the fact that Keynes, in chapters 16 and 17, was hardly at his articulate best. A. C. Pigou called chapter 17 "confused and most confusing," while Joan Robinson referred to it as the "mysterious chapter."[6] Even Keynes himself conceded "the obscurity of this chapter" and suggested that chapters 16 and 17 "do not carry matters to their final destination."[7] It is thus our present purpose to clarify the theoretical framework presented in chapter 17, and in particular to relate Keynes's development of that framework to the Wicksell connection and the Hayek-Sraffa exchange, a task rendered all the more difficult by the fact that, in addition to the "mare's nests and confusions" that abound throughout the book, Keynes himself subsequently offered little by way of clarification.[8] With the notable exceptions of Jacob Viner, Dennis Robertson, and Bertil Ohlin, most of the critics of *The General Theory* went unrebutted by an ill Keynes.[9] As Don Patinkin later observed of *The General Theory*, the fundamental problem is that Keynes "never pulled together its various analytical components into an explicit and complete model: this task was left for its contemporary interpreters."[10]

Our project of unpacking *The General Theory* and relating it to the Wicksell connection will be guided here by what Keynes identified as the key building blocks of his "general theory." Reaffirming other post–*General Theory* recapitulations, in an August 1936 letter to fellow Cantabrigian (and later Keynes biographer) Roy Harrod, in response to the latter's draft review, Keynes listed what he considered the four essential components of *The General Theory*, namely, the concept of effective demand, the psychological law underlying the marginal propensity to consume, liquidity preference, and finally the marginal efficiency of capital.[11] According to the diary of James Meade, Keynes again cited these four elements as the most crucial pieces to *The General Theory* in a March 1945 lecture, just one year before his death.[12] In this chapter, we examine how these four elements fit together to form the second Keynesian variation on the Wicksellian theme, with particular attention paid to the treatment of liquidity preference and the marginal efficiency of capital in chapter 17. After all, in an early draft of *The General Theory*, Keynes suggested that "this book . . . turns mainly on developing a new theory of the relationship between the marginal efficiency of capital and the rate of interest."[13] Chapter 17 is where his four key ingredients are finally brought together to seal this relationship.

The chapter is thus organized as follows. Section 4.1 details Keynes's "own-rates of interest" framework and the concept of the "marginal efficiency of capital"—specifically, how Keynes adapted the Wicksellian money–natural rate concept to a system of multiple "natural" rates of return, à la Sraffa. Section 4.2 then introduces Keynes's own-rates equilibrium and the role of liquidity preference in setting the benchmark for all own-rates of interest. Finally, section 4.3 returns to the Wicksellian cumulative process, and how Keynes's innovative construction of the relationship between liquidity preference and the marginal efficiency of capital resolves the cumulative process into both price and output adjustments.

4.1. OWN-RATES OF INTEREST AND THE MARGINAL EFFICIENCY OF CAPITAL

Chapter 17 is explicitly addressed to the Sraffian critique of Hayek's *Prices and Production*, with Keynes acknowledging Sraffa's review in a footnote on the second page.[14] He furthermore notes that while in *A Treatise* he had defined what he "purported to be a unique rate of interest, which I called the *natural rate* of interest," it was a "mistake to speak of *the* natural rate of interest," there in fact being any number of *different* natural rates, each corresponding to a discrete level of employment. There is thus nothing exclusively "natural" to Wicksell's natural rate, in that while there may be an "*optimum*" rate corresponding to full employment, this rate has no inherent primacy over any other.[15] While Keynes has accordingly absorbed Sraffa's essential point, and Hayek's concession, of the multiplicity of natural rates, he has in fact expanded upon that notion by associating each hypothetical natural rate with a different level of employment. Let us examine how, precisely, he does so.

The basic building block of chapter 17 is Sraffa's commodity rate of interest, which Keynes redubs "own-rate of interest." Evoking Sraffa, he defines the own-rate of interest for any commodity held for investment as merely the difference between the future and spot prices of that commodity in terms of itself, noting that as this delta is "notoriously different for different commodities," there is no reason to suppose the own-rates of any two commodities to be equal.[16] More specifically, each own-rate can be decomposed into three distinct attributes, all measured in terms of the particular commodity itself: a real yield, q, representing some assistance to production or supply of consumer services; a carrying cost, c, encompassing spoilage or "wastage" costs associated with the passage of time; and a liquidity premium, l, referring to the potential nonphysical convenience or security of holding a certain commodity. Thus, the own-rate of interest on any commodity, i, held over a given period is simply its real yield minus its carrying cost plus its liquidity premium, that is, $q_i - c_i + l_i$.[17]

Keynes offers the example of houses, wheat, and money, each possessing a unique own-rate of return. Wheat, with virtually no real yield, a high carrying cost, and limited liquidity, has an own-rate:

$$r_w = - c_w$$

The own-rate for houses, which possess a negligible carrying cost and are highly illiquid but offer a substantial real yield of services, is:

$$r_h = q_h$$

Finally, as money provides no real yield, has a carrying cost of zero, but commands a high liquidity premium owing to exchange value, its own-rate reduces to:

$$r_m = l_m$$

Keynes then implicitly sides with Hayek by demonstrating that, even in equilibrium, these own-rates need not be equivalent; in fact, they may be only by chance, the various *q*'s, *c*'s, and *l*'s of different commodities often being radically different *in natura*. But, again echoing Hayek's reply to Sraffa, Keynes notes that while own-rates will not ordinarily be equivalent in terms of their respective commodities, in equilibrium it must be true that, in terms of any standard commodity, own-rates are equalized; otherwise, markets would be characterized by incomplete arbitrage.[18]

It is worth being pedantic on this point. As Sraffa revealed in his review, we might conceivably choose any commodity as the unit in which all rates of return are denominated, with each standard corresponding to a unique price level. Consequently, because the forward and spot prices of houses in terms of wheat will presumably differ from the forward and spot prices of houses in terms of money, the own-rate of interest of houses in terms of wheat will likewise differ from the house own-rate expressed in terms of money. Keynes, in chapter 17, elaborates Sraffa's argument, writing that "we may take any commodity we choose, e.g. wheat; calculate the wheat-value of the prospective yields of any capital asset; and the rate of discount which makes the present value of this series of wheat annuities equal to the present supply price of the asset in terms of wheat."[19] For any two alternative standards, so long as no change is expected in the relative values of the respective commodities, this rate of discount will be the same. But if one of the alternative standards is expected to change in value relative to the other, the rates of discount on commodities required to bring the present value of future returns into alignment with present supply prices will change by the same percentage. That is, if the two alternative standards under consideration are wheat and money, and wheat is expected to appreciate at a rate of *a* percent per annum in terms of money, then an asset requiring a discount rate of x percent in terms of money will then be $x - a$ percent in terms of wheat.[20]

Before proceeding further, it is necessary to pause, for a moment, to elucidate what Keynes means by this "rate of discount" on a capital asset. The concept is actually derived in chapter 11, "The Marginal Efficiency of Capital," and is listed by Keynes, in his August 30, 1936, letter to Harrod, as one of the four fundamental components of *The General Theory* (the others, recall, being effective demand, the marginal propensity to consume, and liquidity preference). "The proper definition of the marginal efficiency of capital," he writes to Harrod, came "last of all, after an immense lot of muddling and many drafts."[21] Luigi Pasinetti thus calls it a "curious fate" that the product of such laborious "muddling" should have, in subsequent interpretations, been reduced merely to the orthodox notion of the marginal productivity of capital.[22,23]

In standard Neoclassical capital theory, the "marginal productivity of capital" refers to the supposed inverse, monotonic relation between capital per worker and the interest rate. The concept fits conveniently in a standard aggregate production function, in which output is a convex, smooth, differentiable function of "capital" and "labor," with perfect substitutability between factors, and decreasing returns to factor proportions.[24] This is *not*, however, what Keynes meant by the "marginal efficiency of capital." Moreover, he was careful to note "the ambiguity whether we are concerned with the increment of physical product per unit of time due to the employment of one more physical unit of capital, or with the increment of value due to the employment of one more value unit of capital." Keynes's conclusion is that "the former involves difficulties as to the definition of the physical unit of capital, which I believe to be both insoluble and unnecessary."[25] Wicksell would hardly have disagreed.

In contradistinction to a physical product, Keynes thus defines the marginal efficiency of capital as "that rate of discount which would make the present value of the series of annuities given by the returns from the capital-asset during its life just equal to its supply price."[26] In other words, the marginal efficiency of capital describes the relationship between the prospective or expected yield of a particular capital asset, and its current replacement cost.[27] If P_S^j is the present supply price of a capital asset j, and R_t^j the expected net return on the asset in period t, then the marginal efficiency of capital, δ_j, is defined by the following equation:

$$P_S^j = \frac{\sum_{t=1}^{n} R_t^j}{\left(1+\delta_j\right)^t}$$

As Keynes points out, if there is "increased investment in any given type of capital during any period of time, the marginal efficiency of that type of capital will diminish as the investment in it is increased."[28] This will ensue not only because the prospective yield of that particular type of capital will decline as its supply is augmented (the sum of R_t^j's will fall) but also because the increased pressure on supply facilities involved in its production will force a rise in the current replacement cost (P_S^j will increase).

Whether a particular investment project is undertaken, therefore, depends not only upon the state of expectations and current supply prices but also upon the market rate of interest. If $\delta_j > r$, then the investment project will be undertaken; if $\delta_j < r$, it will be abandoned or declined. So long as $\delta_j > r$, investment in that particular project will proceed until, because of either upward pressure on P_S^j or lowered expectations of $\Sigma_{t=1}^{n} R_t^j$, the marginal efficiency of the project is driven to parity with the market rate of interest. According to Keynes, it is therefore possible to construct a schedule indicating by how much investment in a particular capital asset will have to increase in order that its marginal efficiency should fall to any given level. These schedules can then be aggregated "for all the different types of capital, so as to provide a schedule relating the rate of aggregate investment to the corresponding marginal efficiency of capital in general which that rate of investment will establish." It is then evident that investment will be pushed to the point at which "there is no longer any class of capital-asset of which the marginal efficiency exceeds the current rate of interest," that is, until the marginal efficiency of the last profitable investment project is just equal to the prevailing market rate, which is established in the market for existing *financial* assets.[29]

Note the persistence of the Wicksellian voice. Despite Keynes's best efforts to disguise the Wicksell connection, he retains the distinction between a market rate of interest and what is in effect a "natural" rate of return. While the marginal efficiency of capital is different, as we have seen, from Wicksell's natural rate, it does resemble Sraffa's interpretation of the natural rate as the rate of return on some composite commodity. Indeed, Abba Lerner noted that it might be more accurately designated as the "marginal efficiency of investment," since what Keynes is really describing is a complex investment project.[30] Pasinetti suggests that "the concept itself of an investment project is a composite one." That is, "It involves not only existing techniques... but also expectations about possible innovations and about how the techniques may evolve. It involves expectations about new market developments, and new goods."[31] In short, it subsumes Wicksell effects.

The key difference is thus that whereas the Wicksellian equation of the natural rate with the marginal product of "capital" makes technical claims about a marginal relationship ($\partial Q/\partial K$) that can only be measured in value terms, the marginal efficiency of capital aspires to no such assertions. The rate of aggregate investment is inversely related to the marginal efficiency of capital, and thus the rate of interest, *not* because a rise in investment is associated with a substitution of capital for labor when the interest rate falls, *nor* because a fall in the interest rate induces a change in technique from less to more "capital-intensive" production processes, but rather simply because a fall in the rate of interest lowers the marginal efficiency of capital of the *last viable investment project.* As Pasinetti points out, there is "no relation between the 'marginal efficiency' of the last investment project and the *capital-intensity* of the production processes."[32] Rather, the marginal efficiency of capital merely informs us of the *extent* of aggregate investment.

4.2. LIQUIDITY PREFERENCE

Recall that Keynes earlier concluded that *The General Theory* turns mainly on developing a new theory of the relationship between the marginal efficiency of capital and the interest rate. Armed with the preceding conception of the marginal efficiency of capital, Keynes's argument for different "natural" rates of interest corresponding to different levels of aggregate demand, and consequently different levels of employment, thus begins to take shape. He seals the argument in chapter 17, to which we now return, with the own-rates framework adapted from Sraffa's review.

To recapitulate, Sraffa maintained that there is a natural rate of interest that, as a weighted average of the various natural rates entering into some composite commodity (and weighted in the same proportions as the constituent commodities are in the price level itself), will stabilize the price level in terms of that composite commodity.[33] As we have just shown, such a composite natural rate does exist in *The General Theory*: it is the marginal efficiency of capital.[34] Recall, however, that Keynes, in his reply to Hayek's review, claimed that *his* conception of the natural rate was more a "short-period" construct, "taking account of the existing psychology of the market, including errors of forecasting, and irrespective of whether or not the then prevailing rate of investment is expected to be permanent."[35] Keynes retains this vision in his definition and elaboration of the marginal efficiency of capital.

But if the marginal efficiency of capital is a distinctly short-period, contingent variable, it cannot be regarded as a datum. Rather, to determine the point along the marginal efficiency of capital schedule to which investment will be carried, "We must ascertain the rate of interest from some other source, and only then can we value the asset by 'capitalising' its prospective yield."[36] In other words, it is the marginal efficiency of capital, rather than the rate of interest, upon which expectations of changes in nominal prices will operate. This requires that investment in a capital asset with a marginal efficiency unequal to the prevailing market rate of interest must be scaled either up or down until its yield has been driven to parity, or else that the asset must appreciate or depreciate in terms of some other commodity serving as numéraire.[37]

Keynes thus sets out to establish why it is the own-rate of interest on money that will determine the rate to which the marginal efficiency of capital must rise or fall. Assigning money the role of numéraire, he accordingly includes an appreciation factor "*a*" in his own-rates equation to account for "what the changes in relative values during the year are expected to be." That is, "*a*" is "the percentage appreciation (or depreciation)" of each commodity in terms of that standard in which prices are reckoned, namely, money.[38] Thus, if the commodity own-rate in terms of commodity *i* is:

$$r_i = q_i - c_i + l_i$$

then the same own-rate in terms of money, what Keynes terms the "own-rate of money-interest," will be:

$$r_{i,m} = q_i - c_i + l_i + a_i$$

with a_i representing the expected percentage increase in the value of commodity *i* relative to money, or:

$$a_i = \frac{P^i_{f,m} - P^i_{s,m}}{P^i_{s,m}}$$

where $P^i_{s,m}$ and $P^i_{f,m}$ represent the spot and future exchange values of commodity *i* relative to money.

In equilibrium, while own-rates of interest may remain unique, it must nonetheless be the case that own-rates of money-interest will converge, in order that "there is nothing to choose in the way of advantage between the alternatives."[39] Returning to Keynes's simple example, therefore, we see that if wheat, house, and money own-rates of money-interest are, respectively:

$$r_{w,m} = a_w - c_w$$

$$r_{h,m} = q_h + a_h$$

$$r_{m,m} = l_m$$

then market equilibrium will obtain when the own-rates of money-interest on each commodity, including money, are equalized, such that:

$$r_{w,m} = r_{h,m} = r_{m,m}$$

or,

$$a_w - c_w = q_h + a_h = l_m$$

For each capital asset j, it must also therefore be true that the marginal efficiency of that asset, δ_j, when expressed in money terms, must align with all other own-rates of money-interest, including the money own-rate of money-interest. That is:

$$\delta_{j,m} = a_w - c_w = q_h + a_h = l_m$$

where

$$\delta_{j,m} = q_j - c_j + l_j + a_j$$

It should be immediately apparent that the various q's, c's, l's, and a's will have to adjust in some fashion, but to which equality? The answer is not entirely obvious. Here, then, Keynes identifies those "peculiarities" of the money-rate of interest that, he claims, dictate not only why it will likely be the greatest of the own-rates but also why it will ordinarily serve as the own-rate that "rules the roost."[40] The peculiarities, Keynes argues, are to be found in the "essential properties" of money itself.

The first essential property of money is that, unlike most other assets, money has a negligible elasticity of production. That is, "Labour cannot be turned on at will by entrepreneurs to produce money in increasing quantities as its price rises."[41] Second, money "has an elasticity of substitution equal, or nearly equal, to zero," which means "there is no tendency to substitute some other factor for it" when the price of money rises.[42] Finally, as the standard of value, money is unique in its capacity to offer "immediate, liquid command" over goods and services. The nonmonetary asset holder must be "prepared to part with immediate command for a specified or indefinite period, leaving it to future market conditions to determine on what terms he can, if necessary, convert deferred commands over specific goods into immediate command over goods in general." But the same is not true of money, for which goods and services are readily exchanged in both current and future periods. It is for this reason that money may command a liquidity premium very much in excess of its carrying costs, which are effectively nil.[43]

The third property of money thus explains why asset demand may be "predominantly directed to money," the first that if this occurs labor cannot be employed in producing more money, and the second that no other asset can be called forth to assume money's role.[44] Together, these three properties constitute the decisive factors in Keynes's asset market equilibrium. As we have already seen, those assets of which the marginal efficiency would be greater than the market rate of interest (i.e., those assets "of which the normal supply-price is less than the demand-price") will be newly produced. But as the stock of these assets is increased, their marginal efficiency will decline. As Keynes concludes, "Thus a point will come at which it no longer pays to produce them, *unless the rate of interest falls* pari passu."[45]

If, therefore, "there is some asset (e.g. money) of which the rate of interest is fixed (or declines more slowly as output increases than does any other commodity's rate of interest), how is the position adjusted?"[46] The answer is that all other own-rates of money-interest will have to rise accordingly, through some adjustment of the various *q*'s, *c*'s, *l*'s, and *a*'s. The fundamental point, however, is that it will in this case be the greatest of the own-rates that determines equilibrium, and since money is distinguished by the fact that, unlike capital assets, demand for it cannot call forth greater production or substitution, it will ordinarily be the money own-rate that is the greatest of the own-rates, and consequently the one that "rules the roost."[47] That is, it is the money own-rate of money-interest that will determine how far down the marginal efficiency of capital schedule investment can be pushed. Thus, a decline in the marginal efficiency of capital to parity with the market rate of interest corresponds to the extension and/or reorganization of existing capital projects, and/or the introduction of new ones, up to the point at which all own money own-rates of return are equal and there is thus no pressure on spot and forward prices to adjust further.

4.3. THE CUMULATIVE PROCESS

With the vital "relationship between the marginal efficiency of capital and the rate of interest" in mind, let us turn then, to Keynes's final iteration of the Wicksellian cumulative process. As in *A Treatise*, Keynes's primary concern in *The General Theory* is one of deflation, rather than inflation. Once again, it is the divergence between market and natural rates of interest (though Keynes has avoided these exact terms) that constitutes the mainspring of change. In *The General Theory*, this means a fall in the marginal efficiency of capital corresponding to an inward shift of the investment demand schedule, from I_0 to I_1, as shown in Figure 4.3.1. While it is conceivable for this initial equilibrium to be disturbed by a sudden fluctuation in the rate of interest, or else due to capital saturation, for the sake of exposition we will here adopt the position of the "Chapter 12 Keynesians" in supposing disruption to emanate rather from a shift in the investment demand (i.e., marginal efficiency of capital) schedule, owing to an adverse shock to long-term expectations. After all, as Keynes notes in chapter 12, "The State of Long-Term Expectation," "The schedule of the marginal efficiency of capital is of fundamental importance because it is mainly through this factor

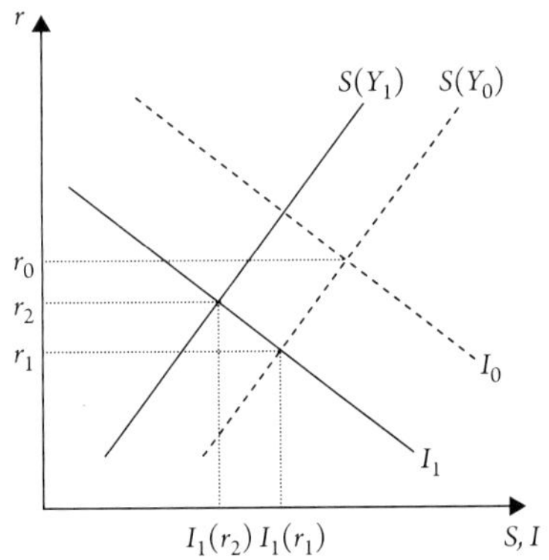

Figure 4.3.1 Credit: J. M. Keynes, *The General Theory of Employment, Interest, and Money* (1936; reprint, New York: Harcourt, Brace, 1965), 180.

(much more than through the rate of interest) that the expectation of the future influences the present."[48]

In *A Treatise*, this shift generated an excess supply of loanable funds at the original rate of interest, r_0, with bearish speculators (in Wicksell and Hayek's case, the banks) absorbing surplus cash holdings. So long as Keynes's speculators were willing to replace income-earning assets with cash, (nominal) output would remain depressed. But, eventually, deflationary pressures would cumulate, forcing the money rate into line with the new natural rate *at full employment*. Critically, the process was still self-equilibrating in *A Treatise*, and the mechanism of equilibration was nominal adjustments eventually forcing a close of the saving-investment gap; output fluctuations were a distinctly ad hoc theoretical affair.

Borrowing the language of *A Treatise*, we might again note that at the *old* equilibrium rate of interest, r_0, there now exists, on impact, an excess supply of commodities in the amount of $S(Y_0) - I_1(r_0)$. In other words, savers intend to accumulate income-earning securities at the rate $S(Y_0)$, whereas firms intend to float new securities only at the rate $I_1(r_0)$.[49] As a result of this deficit in the planned flow supply of new securities, prices of existing securities *should* be immediately bid up, while the simultaneous excess supply of commodities *should* exert instantaneous downward pressure on consumer prices. From a purely asset-market perspective, investors, in perfect anticipation of rising asset prices, *should* release cash from idle balances in order to purchase income-bearing securities. Assuming agents act as they "should," the rate of interest *will* immediately fall to its new equilibrium level of r_1, such that $S(Y_1) = I_1(r_1)$. Provided all transactors act in the manner that the new full-employment equilibrium requires of them, that is, the actual rate of interest will track the equilibrium rate pari passu. Consumption demand will rise by $S(Y_0) - S(Y_1)$, and demand for capital goods by $I_1(r_1) - I_1(r_0)$, thereby nipping any notional excess demand for securities, and excess supply of commodities, in the bud.

Leijonhufvud argues that the key innovation of *The General Theory* relative to the *Treatise* model is that by imposing the $S = I$ identity and integrating Kahn's multiplier, Keynes is able to affix quantity adjustments to his cumulative process.[50] The interest rate, rather than performing the task of coordinating saving and investment, is instead busy clearing the market for *existing* assets according to liquidity preference, as we have just seen, and can thus play no role in bringing saving and investment into line (after all, if saving is identically equal to investment, then the interest rate has no business coordinating the two).

Thus, now, the fall in investment, through the multiplier effect, reduces aggregate demand from Y_0 to Y_1. r_1 is hence the new "natural" rate, corresponding to the marginal efficiency of capital consistent with full employment, which would prevail if saving remained constant. But at the new level of income, saving will not remain constant; when investment shifts, so too does income (since $Y = C + I$), and thus so too does the volume of saving out of a given level of income. That is, when investment changes, saving is brought automatically into equality by the operation of the multiplier, which is in turn determined by the marginal propensity to consume.

Meanwhile, the interest rate, as Leijonhufvud is keen to stress, plays no part in this sequence; while income adjustments equilibrate saving and investment, the interest rate is busy in the market for existing assets, in accordance with our analysis of chapter 17. Though the immediate consequence of the adverse investment demand shock is an excess of intended saving over intended investment at the given initial levels of income and rate of interest, the immanent gap can only be closed by a multiplier-induced fall in aggregate demand. The savings supply curve therefore shifts inward from $S(Y_0)$ to $S(Y_1)$, such that saving-investment equilibrium occurs at a rate of interest, say, r_2, above the new natural rate. Conceivably, r_2 could even get stuck at r_0, with the attendant further decline in output. The important difference here, as compared with *A Treatise* (and, indeed, as compared with Wicksell and Hayek), is that the loanable funds market clears; there are no bearish speculators required to sustain r_2 above r_1.[51]

In fact, because of the multiplier effect, r_2 settles at a point below full employment, with *no tendency to adjust further.* The loanable funds market is in equilibrium; the money market is in equilibrium; the only market that remains out of equilibrium is the labor market. While lower output will place some pressure on the money wage, there is no reason to expect the wage rate to decline—it is the interest rate that constitutes the "wrong" price here.[52] Moreover, if the problem is our standard Wicksellian one of a misalignment of saving and investment that requires a rise in consumption to resolve without sacrificing employment, reducing wage income will not constitute a solution. With the rate of interest stuck above r_1, there is simply no determinative pressure toward full employment.

On this point Keynes is emphatic. Referring back to *A Treatise*, he notes that he had then employed the idea of a "Wicksellian" natural rate "which preserved equality between the rate of savings... and the rate of investment." In so doing, he had, "however, overlooked the fact that in any given society there is, on this definition, a *different* natural rate of interest for each hypothetical level of employment." In *The General Theory*, savings *always* equals investment ("forced saving" is out the door); the rate of interest, by regulating the marginal efficiency of capital, simply determines the level of output at which savings and investment are equalized. "Thus it was a mistake," Keynes concludes, "to speak of the natural rate of interest or to suggest that the above definition would yield a unique value for the rate of interest irrespective of the level of employment. I had not then understood that, in certain conditions, the system could be in equilibrium with less than full employment."[53] Paying lip service to Wicksell, he then declares:

> I am no longer of the opinion that the concept of a "natural" rate of interest, which previously seemed to me a most promising idea, has anything very useful or significant to contribute to our analysis. It is merely the rate of interest which will preserve the *status quo*; and in general, we have no predominant interest in the *status quo* as such.[54]

In other words, when the marginal efficiency of capital schedule shifts, so too does the rate of interest that would maintain the original level of employment and income. Moreover, if employment and income change, then the rate that would have sustained the original equilibrium instantly loses any attractive force.[55]

To be sure, deflation and falling income will produce an excess supply of money at the old rate, but this will merely have the effect of driving down the interest rate to the point at which excess cash balances will be voluntarily held, given the state of liquidity preference. Though the interest rate may be "wrong," in the sense of being inconsistent with the vector of prices that would obtain at full-employment equilibrium, with saving equal to investment, there is no systemic pressure on investors to revise this "wrong" price in the "right" direction.[56] And nor should we expect flexible money wages or broad-based deflation to do the trick; with respect to the vector of full-employment equilibrium prices, wages are at their "correct" level. With the interest rate remaining at a level inconsistent with full-employment equilibrium, it is intertemporal prices—specifically, the ratio of investment to consumer goods prices—that are thus off their mark, and general deflation can do nothing to resolve a problem of relative prices.[57] Basically, so long as the interest rate is not at its full-employment level, unemployment will not tend toward its full-employment, natural level.[58] Indeed, unloading the burden of adjustment onto wages and the absolute price level may only compound the confusion.

This point is driven home by Keynes's colleague Roy Harrod, who writes that "the theory of interest is, I think, the central point in [Keynes's] scheme." He continues:

> [Keynes] departs from old orthodoxy in holding that the failure of the system to move to a position of full activity is not primarily due to friction, rigidity, immobility or to phenomena essentially connected with the trade cycle. If a certain level of interest is established which is inconsistent with full activity, no flexibility or mobility in the other parts of the system will get the system to move to full activity. *But this wrong rate of interest, as we may call it, is not itself a rigidity or inflexibility. It is natural, durable, and in a certain sense in the free system inevitable.*[59]

It is true that nominal wage rigidity (or any other nominal rigidity, for that matter), may appear the offender, in that wages would have to adjust to achieve consistency with full employment. But while it may be the case that so long as the interest rate is at its full-employment, natural level, employment will tend toward its full-employment, natural level, the same, to repeat, is not true in reverse.

It should by now be clear how Keynes justifies this claim. Recall that he explicitly linked the marginal efficiency of capital, and thus investment demand, to the rate of interest by noting that "those assets of which the normal supply-price is less than the demand-price will be newly produced; and these will be those assets of which the marginal efficiency would be greater (on the basis of their normal supply-price) than the rate of interest."[60] Consequently, if the economy is faced with a liquidity premium on money which refuses to decline pari passu with the marginal efficiency of capital, investment will have to be scaled back until the marginal efficiency of capital is pushed up to parity with the money own-rate of money interest. This, of course, unleashes Kahn's multiplier, and hence the underemployment dynamics outlined earlier.

The multiplier, however, can only come into play if, and only if, relative money prices fail to adjust with sufficient speed. This is, in fact, precisely why it is valid to say that *The General Theory* still functions within the Wicksellian natural rate framework. For it is still possible to transition from one, higher natural rate to another, lower one, consistent with full employment, *provided* investors are able to perceive immediately a shift in the marginal efficiency of capital. In other words, if the various "*a*" terms in Keynes's own-rates equation adjust instantaneously in response to the relative rise in liquidity preference, money prices will bear the full brunt of adjustment. For example, suppose the marginal efficiency of capital asset *j*, in money terms, is:

$$\delta_{j,m} = q_j - c_j + l_j + \left(\frac{P^j_{f,m} - P^j_{s,m}}{P^j_{s,m}} \right)$$

and that we are in asset market equilibrium, such that $\delta_{j,m} = l_m$. If l_m then rises relatively and, as per the properties of money, refuses to decline, there is no unqualified reason why q_j, rather than a_j, must bear the burden. In a full-information context, the rise in l_m should merely coincide with investors selling money forward to buy it spot. In other words, the spot money price of any commodity or capital asset, $P^j_{s,m}$, should fall, and the future money price, $P^j_{f,m}$, rise; real assets should be expected to appreciate in terms of money. If $P^j_{s,m}$ would merely fall relative to $P^j_{f,m}$, proportionately to the rise in l_m, then the marginal efficiency of capital would rise to parity with the money rate of interest with no required contraction in real investment. That is, real yields, q_j, might remain invariant. In terms of the marginal efficiency of capital, we would simply expect present replacement costs in terms of money to fall relative to the net present value of future returns in terms of money. Real relative prices being unchanged, there should thus be no reason why an investment project that was previously viable at full employment should subsequently be rendered unprofitable merely because the value of money has risen.

Here, then, is where neo-Walrasian confusion creeps in. For a cursory reading of chapter 17 might indeed suggest that the culprit is none other than nominal price stickiness; *if only* spot prices of capital assets in terms of money would fall appropriately (or else expectations of future money prices rise), investment would not have to contract, there would be no multiplier effect, and hence no unemployment equilibrium.[61] But this conclusion misses the very substance of chapter 17; for we might just as appropriately ask: Why *should* money prices adjust? The raison d'être for a standard of value, after all, is that prices in terms of that standard are expected to remain stable.[62] Thus, if a producer finds demand for his product falling short of original expectations, why should we suppose him to respond first with adjustment of money prices, as opposed to drawing down inventory?[63] Nominal prices *ought* to be sticky.

If, Keynes argues, real relative prices were indeed the primary source of stability in the economy, the effect "could only be to cause a violent oscillation of money-prices. For every small fluctuation in the propensity to consume and the inducement to invest would cause money-prices to rush violently between zero and infinity." That nominal prices should be more stable than real ones "is a condition of the system possessing inherent stability."[64,65] Moreover, the trouble is not simply that spot prices in terms of money must fall; they must fall *relative to* forward money prices. If a decline in the marginal efficiency of capital relative to the liquidity premium of money is to be accommodated purely via adjustments in Keynes's "*a*" terms, then $P^j_{s,m}$ must fall without dragging $P^j_{f,m}$ down with it. But this, crucially, will depend upon the state of expectations; if spot money prices are to fall relative to future money prices, then investors must expect capital assets to appreciate against the standard of value at a faster rate than previously.[66] In other words, future expectations must be immune to current nominal deflation. If they are not, the door is flung open to the multiplier.

The problem, in fact, is greater still. For the breakdown of the interest rate mechanism is not just a failure of relative nominal price adjustment but constitutes also, on impact, an effective demand failure. If the interest rate is wrong, then supplied investment goods and capital assets cannot all find their own demands, and thus are not perfectly liquid. Agents are consequently subject to quantity as well as price constraints, and thus, to borrow Clower's terms, "effective demand" may fall below "notional" demand. According to Keynes, "effective demand" is the "income (or proceeds) which the entrepreneurs expect to receive, inclusive of the incomes which they will hand on to the other factors of production, from the amount of current employment which they decide to give."[67] The trouble is that if prices are "wrong," in the sense that they are inconsistent with the new equilibrium at r_1, then not all supplied goods and services are effectively demanded. That is, there is a fall in effective demand; demands for some goods and services cannot be funded by supplies of other goods and services.[68] Money, therefore, far from being a neutral veil, acquires the ability to constrain expenditure. If money prices are wrong, then sellers of goods whose money prices are too high will be constrained in their purchases of other goods by money income actually realized. The standard Neoclassical ranking of adjustment velocities is thereby inverted; thwarted price adjustments give way to income-constrained quantity adjustments.

This dynamic is what Clower dubbed the "dual decision hypothesis" of *The General Theory*—if prices diverge from their full-employment equilibrium values, effective demand diverges from notional demand, and Walrasian-style price *tâtonnement* is joined by quantity adjustments. As Leijonhufvud puts it, "*Realized transaction quantities* enter as arguments of the excess demand functions in addition to prices."[69] The difficulty, however, is that allied to Keynes's multiplier, quantity adjustments have a deviation-amplifying effect. A reduction in effective demand in any one product or asset (owing to the wealth effect) market has, via the marginal propensity to consume, further multiplier effects on income, and thus consumption, in other markets, thereby adversely redounding upon demand in the aggregate. Rather than deviation-counteracting price adjustments steering the economy to full-employment equilibrium, price-cum-quantity adjustments have the effect of cumulatively driving the economy *away* from full-employment equilibrium.

The Wicksell connection may by this point seem somewhat difficult to discern. It is present nonetheless. The source of the confusion is that Keynes has heavily disguised Wicksell's natural rate. Certainly, once the multiplier gets a foot in the door, it is possible to conceive of multiple natural rates corresponding to different levels of employment. But there is still a natural rate associated with full employment; it is simply the marginal efficiency of the last profitable investment process consistent with the entire set of intertemporal prices established *at full employment*. The key question—and this is where Keynes makes a decisive break from Wicksell—is whether that rate has any attractive durability once the market rate departs from it. If liquidity preference joins forces with effective demand failure and the multiplier, Keynes's answer: unlikely.

There is more, however, to the Keynesian variation on the Wicksellian theme, namely, the definition of the marginal efficiency of capital itself. It is not merely Wicksell's natural rate by another name. For Keynes, what is important is not whether a particular process will produce a greater physical yield, given that it is lengthy or otherwise "capital-intensive," but rather whether the process under consideration is "so organised as to produce in the most efficient manner *compatible with delivery at the dates at which consumer's demand is expected to become effective*."[70] Ultimately, it is the value of output forthcoming from an investment project at the appropriate points in time that is of primary concern, as it is entirely conceivable that the value of output will decrease as more "roundabout" investment processes are undertaken, even though their physical efficiency may be still increasing.[71] The challenge facing the economic agent, then, is that he must make contracts today to fund capital projects—to build factories, acquire inventory, or invest in research and development—the output of which will only mature under circumstances he can neither know nor, in the absence of statistical certainty equivalents, effectively hedge against.

Keynes elaborates this point with a creative analogy in chapter 16, "Sundry Observations on the Nature of Capital":

> If, after hearing full particulars of the meals he can get by fixing dinner at different hours, the consumer is expected to decide in favour of 8 o'clock, it is the business of the cook to provide the best dinner he can for service at that hour, irrespective of

> whether 7.30, 8 o'clock or 8.30 is the hour which would suit him best if time counted for nothing, one way or the other, and his only task was to produce the absolutely best dinner.[72]

In all of *The General Theory*, perhaps no passage better encapsulates Keynes's fusion of his four ingredients. For if an entrepreneur undertakes an investment project on the basis of its prospective yield, and subsequently finds demand for his output lacking, then he will be inclined either to scale back the investment or otherwise reorganize it so as to deliver the desired outputs at the desired dates. In this, a stable standard of value may, far from being an obstruction to market forces, in fact prove instrumental in coordinating output adjustments.

The problem is if the standard of value itself is mispriced. Leijonhufvud suggests that any theory incorporating liquidity preference "will attach a *probability of zero*" to a successful traverse from one full-employment growth path to another, "for the simple reason that the only price mechanism that might do it never gets into play to coordinate saving and investment decisions."[73] Based upon our analysis of chapter 17, this conclusion is not entirely accurate; the probability may be slight, but it is non-trivial. The economy can and may effect the traverse *if* relative prices (the various a_i terms) adjust; the caveat, as per the Wicksellian tradition, is that savers, speculators, and entrepreneurs must act upon consistent expectations of future prospects.[74] If they do not, relative prices will be "wrong," intertemporal prices "wrong," and the task of own-rates equilibration shifted from the a_i to the q_i terms.

NOTES

1. Axel Leijonhufvud, "The Wicksell Connection: Variations on a Theme," in *Information and Coordination: Essays in Macroeconomic Theory* (New York: Oxford University Press, 1981), 134.

2. A. H. Hansen, *A Guide to Keynes* (New York: McGraw-Hill, 1953), 155, 159. The fact that Hansen would choose to overlook chapter 17, with its Wicksellian roots, might indeed explain why the Keynesian "revolution" would soon fall victim to the imperializing aspirations of neo-Walrasian general equilibrium.
3. M. Blaug, *Economic Theory in Retrospect*, 3d ed. (Cambridge: Cambridge University Press, 1978), 658.
4. Since the publication of *The General Theory*, and particularly since the 1980s, chapter 17 has in fact been the subject of considerable debate. For various interpretations and analyses, see H. Townshend, "Liquidity-Premium and the Theory of Value," *Economic Journal* 47 (1937): 157–169; A. P. Lerner, "The Essential Properties of Interest and Money," *Quarterly Journal of Economics* 66 (1952): 172–193; A. H. Hansen, *A Guide to Keynes* (New York: McGraw-Hill, 1953); J. W. Conard, *An Introduction to the Theory of Interest* (Berkeley: University of California Press, 1959); N. Kaldor, "Keynes's Theory of Own-Rates of Interest," in *Essays on Economic Stability and Growth*, ed. N. Kaldor (London: Duckworth, 1960); A. P. Lerner, "Own-Rates and the Liquidity Trap," *Economic Journal* 72 (1962): 449–452; R. Turvey, "Does the Rate of Interest Rule the Roost?," in *The Theory of the Rate of Interest*, ed. F. Hahn and F. P. R. Brechling (London: Macmillan, 1965); C. J. Bliss, "Equal Rates of Profit," in *The New Palgrave: A Dictionary of Economics*, ed. J. Eatwell, M. Milgate, and P. Newman, vol. 2 (London: Macmillan, 1987); A. Cottrell and M. S. Lawlor, "'Natural Rate' Mutations: Keynes, Leijonhufvud and the Wicksell Connection," *History of Political Economy* 23 (1991): 625–643; T. Cowen and R. Kroszner, "Money's Marketability Premium and the Microfoundations of Keynes's Theory of Money and Interest," *Cambridge Journal of Economics* 18 (1994): 379–390; H. Garretsen, *Keynes, Coordination and Beyond: The Development of Macroeconomics and Monetary Theory since 1945* (Aldershot: Edward Elgar, 1992); J. A. Kregel, "Money, Expectations and Relative Prices in Keynes' Monetary Equilibrium," *Economie Appliquée* 35 (1982): 449–465; J. A. Kregel, "Hamlet without the Prince: Cambridge Macroeconomics without Money," *American Economic Review* 75 (1985): 133–139; J. A. Kregel, "The Multiplier and Liquidity Preference: Two Sides of the Theory of Demand," in *The Foundations of Keynesian Analysis*, ed. A. Barrère (London: Macmillan, 1988); M. S. Lawlor, *The Economics of Keynes in Historical Context* (New York: Palgrave Macmillan, 2006); F. C. Maclachlan, *Keynes's General Theory of Interest: A Reconsideration* (London: Routledge, 1993); C. Panico, "The Evolution of Keynes's Thought on the Rate of Interest," *Contributions to Political Economy* 6 (1987): 53–61; C. Rogers, *Money, Interest and Capital* (Cambridge: Cambridge University Press, 1989); J. Runde, "Keynesian Uncertainty and Liquidity Preference," *Cambridge Journal of Economics* 18 (1994): 129–144; I. Barens and V. Caspari, "Own-Rates of Interest and Their Relevance for the Existence of Underemployment Equilibrium Positions," in *A "Second Edition"*

of The General Theory, ed. G. C. Harcourt and P. A. Riach, vol. 1 (London: Routledge, 1997); J. A. Kregel, "The Theory of Value, Expectations and Chapter 17 of *The General Theory*," in *A "Second Edition" of* The General Theory, ed. G. C. Harcourt and P. A. Riach, vol. 1 (London: Routledge, 1997).

5. And it should also then come as no surprise that the internecine warfare between fundamentalist and orthodox Keynesians over capital theory and the Phillips curve was subsequently waged so intensely.
6. A. C. Pigou, "Mr. J. M. Keynes' *General Theory of Employment, Interest and Money*," *Economica* 3 (1936): 125; J. V. Robinson, "Own-Rates of Interest," *Economic Journal* 71 (1961): 596.
7. J. M. Keynes to D. H. Robertson, February 20, 1935, in *The Collected Writings of John Maynard Keynes*, ed. D. E. Moggridge, vol. 13, *The General Theory and After, Part I: Preparation* (London: Macmillan, 1973), 519; J. M. Keynes, *The Collected Writings of John Maynard Keynes*, ed. D. E. Moggridge, vol. 29, *The General Theory and After: A Supplement* (London: Macmillan, 1973), 213–214.
8. Quotation from Paul Samuelson, "The General Theory," in *Keynes's "General Theory": Reports of Three Decades*, ed. R. Lekachman (London: Macmillan, 1964), 318–319.
9. This was largely due to the decline in Keynes's health around 1938, followed by his subsequent intense work at The Treasury during the war.
10. Don Patinkin, "On Different Interpretations of the *General Theory*," in *John Maynard Keynes: Critical Assessments*, ed. John Cunningham, vol. 8 (London: Routledge, 1994), 243.
11. J. M. Keynes to R. F. Harrod, August 30, 1936, in *The Collected Writings of John Maynard Keynes*, ed. D. E. Moggridge, vol. 14, *The General Theory and After, Part II: Defence and Development* (London: Macmillan, 1973), 85. See also Keynes's lecture notes for this occasion: J. M. Keynes, *Collected Writings*, vol. 27, 388n; cited in Patinkin, "On Different Interpretations," 248n.
12. J. E. Meade, *The Cabinet Office Diary: 1944–1946*, in *The Collected Papers of James Meade*, ed. Susan Howson and Donald Moggridge, vol. 6 (London: Unwin Hyman, 1990).
13. Keynes, *Collected Writings*, 14:362.
14. J. M. Keynes, *General Theory of Employment, Interest and Money* (1936; reprint, Cambridge: Cambridge University Press, 1973), 223.
15. Ibid., 242–243.
16. Ibid., 223.
17. Ibid., 225–226.
18. Another way to put this is that in equilibrium there must be a set of relative price ratios such that there exist no opportunities for arbitrage. For example, if houses, currently exchanging for wheat at a ratio of ρ_1, are one year hence to exchange at a ratio of ρ_2, where $\rho_2 < \rho_1$, then the house own-rate of interest in terms of wheat must reflect the expected appreciation in the value of houses relative to wheat.

19. Keynes, *General Theory*, 224.
20. Ibid.
21. Keynes to Harrod, *Collected Writings*, 14:85.
22. Luigi Pasinetti, "The Marginal Efficiency of Investment," in *A "Second Edition" of* The General Theory, ed. G. C. Harcourt and P. A. Riach, vol. 1 (London: Routledge, 1997), 198. For an early (mis)interpretation of the "marginal efficiency of capital," see, for example, J. R. Hicks, "Mr. Keynes and the 'Classics': A Suggested Interpretation," *Econometrica* 5 (1937): 147–159.
23. The fate of the marginal efficiency of capital may not be so curious when we consider that Lord Kahn, whom Keynes recognized as the most important influence on *The General Theory*, called chapter 11 "the most important" but also "one of the most confused." Evidently chapters 11 and 17 have both been the source of persistent confusion. Richard Kahn, *The Making of Keynes's "General Theory"* (Cambridge: Cambridge University Press, 1984), 145.
24. Pasinetti, "The Marginal Efficiency of Investment," 199.
25. Keynes, *General Theory*, 138.
26. Ibid., 135. In modern parlance, we might call this the "internal rate of return."
27. Keynes defines the "supply price" of a capital asset as "not the market-price at which an asset of the type in question can actually be purchased in the market, but the price which would just induce a manufacturer newly to produce an additional unit of such assets, i.e. what is sometimes called its *replacement cost*." Ibid.
28. Ibid., 136.
29. Ibid., 136–137. See also Pasinetti, "The Marginal Efficiency of Investment," 198–218.
30. A. P. Lerner, "On the Marginal Product of Capital and the Marginal Efficiency of Investment," *Journal of Political Economy* 61 (1953): 1–14. For more on Keynes's marginal efficiency of capital and its interpretation, see A. Alchian, "The Rate of Interest, Fisher's Rate of Return over Cost, and Keynes' Internal Rate of Return," *American Economic Review* 45 (1955): 938–943; A. Asimakopulos, "The Determination of Investment in Keynes's Model," *Canadian Journal of Economics* 4 (1971): 382–388; P. Garegnani, "Notes on Consumption, Investment and Effective Demand: I," *Cambridge Journal of Economics* 2 (1978): 335–353; P. Garegnani, "Notes on Consumption, Investment and Effective Demand: II," *Cambridge Journal of Economics* 3 (1979): 63–82; J. Hirshleifer, "On the Theory of the Optimal Investment Decision," *Journal of Political Economy* 66 (1958): 329–352; M. Kalecki, "The Principle of Increasing Risk," *Economica* 4 (1937): 440–447; P. Davidson, *Money and the Real World* (New York: Halstead, 1972); H. P. Minsky, *John Maynard Keynes* (New York: Columbia University Press, 1975).
31. Pasinetti, "The Marginal Efficiency of Investment," 206.
32. Ibid., 207.
33. Piero Sraffa, "Dr. Hayek on Money and Capital," *Economic Journal* 42 (1932): 51.

34. Ludwig Lachmann, *Capital and Its Structure* (London: Bell and Sons, 1956), 76–77. Heinz Kurz raises objections both to Keynes's investment and liquidity preference theories and to relating Keynes's ideas to Sraffa's concept of the "standard commodity." See Heinz D. Kurz, "Keynes, Sraffa, and the Latter's 'Secret Skepticism,'" in *The Return to Keynes*, ed. Bradley Bateman, Toshiaka Hirai, and Maria Cristina Marcuzzo (Cambridge, MA: Harvard University Press, 2010), 184–204. Also, C. Panico, "Monetary Analyses in Sraffa's Writings," in *Piero Sraffa's Political Economy: A Centenary Estimate*, ed. Terenzio Cozzi and Roberto Marchionatti (London: Routledge, 2001).
35. J. M. Keynes, "The Pure Theory of Money: A Reply to Dr. Hayek," *Economica* 11 (November 1931): 395.
36. Keynes, *General Theory*, 137.
37. Ibid., 224–225.
38. Ibid., 227.
39. Ibid., 227–228.
40. Ibid., 223, 229.
41. Ibid., 230.
42. Ibid., 231.
43. Moreover, it is the very fact that the future direction of prices, and thus rates of interest, is uncertain that asset holders are willing to forgo real yield to secure additional liquidity. Given the exceptional liquidity of money, "*uncertainty* as to the future course of the rate of interest is the sole intelligible explanation of the type of liquidity preference... which leads to the holding of cash." Ibid., 201.
44. Ibid., 234. Keynes does acknowledge that some "relief" may come in the form of the real-balances effect. He dismisses this argument, however, on account of the properties of money, noting that "the fact that money has low elasticities of production and substitution and low carrying-costs tends to raise the expectation that money-wages will be relatively stable; and this expectation enhances money's liquidity-premium." Ibid., 238. For more on Keynes and the real-balances effect see, for example, Hicks, "Mr. Keynes and the 'Classics,'" 147–159; A.C. Pigou, "The Classical Stationary State," *Economic Journal* 53 (1943): 343–351; D. Patinkin, "Price Flexibility and Full Employment," *American Economic Review* 38 (1948): 543–564; J. Tobin, "The Interest Elasticity of the Transactions Demand for Cash," *Review of Economic Studies* 23 (1956): 241–247.
45. Keynes, *General Theory*, 228 (emphasis in original).
46. Ibid.
47. Ibid., 223, 234–235. Essentially, the adjustment mechanisms of capital-asset own-rates are inapplicable to money. By ascertaining the rate of interest from another source, namely, liquidity preference, Keynes thus in effect inverts the Wicksellian cumulative process. In his new schema, it is the marginal efficiency of capital that must adjust to a fixed money rate, not the other way around.

48. Keynes, *The General Theory*, 145.
49. In essence, the supply of savings (demand for securities), $SY_0(Y_0)$, exceeds investment demand (supply of securities), $I_1(r_0)$, keeping in mind that these are *planned* magnitudes. See Leijonhufvud, "The Wicksell Connection," 161–162.
50. Ibid., 170.
51. Ibid., 171–172.
52. Ibid., 167.
53. Keynes, *The General Theory*, 242.
54. Ibid., 243.
55. This point is illustrated by the only graph appearing in *The General Theory* (reproduced here), which Keynes included only upon Harrod's suggestion. Suppose, with Keynes, that the economy begins at a point such as the intersection of Y_1 (saving out of total income) and X_1X_1' (investment demand), corresponding to interest rate r_1. While it might be the case that, in the event of an inward shift of the investment demand schedule, from X_1X_1' to X_2X_2', an interest rate of r_2 would equate saving and investment at the initial level of output, inasmuch as the interest rate fails to *immediately* fall to r_2, Y_1 will with equal immediacy be rendered irrelevant. When the investment demand schedule shifts, income will, in general, shift too, which means, with a given marginal propensity to consume, saving will fall alongside investment. The re-equilibrating price pressures of excess savings are thus foiled before they can even exert themselves. By how much income falls will be determined by the size of the multiplier and the extent of adjustment on the part of the rate of interest, which depends, crucially, on liquidity preference. But the bottom line is that once the interest rate has failed to adjust, there may be no forces at work pulling the economy to a full-employment equilibrium, be it in the short run, long run, or any run.

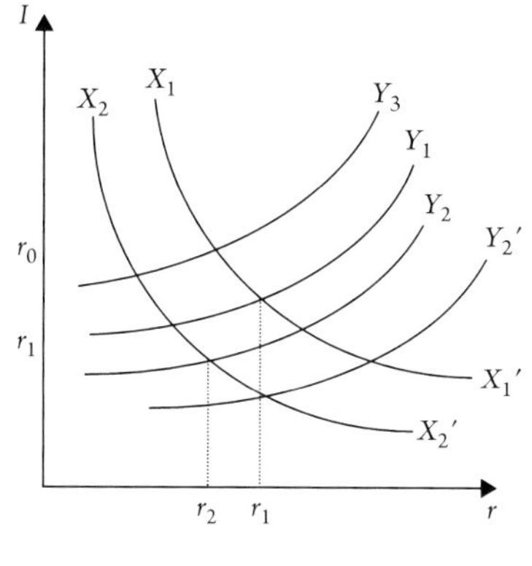

Keynes, *The General Theory*, 180–181.
56. Ibid., 166.
57. Ibid., 191–192.
58. Leijonhufvud, "The Wicksell Connection," 185.
59. Roy Harrod, "Keynes the Economist," in *The New Economics*, ed. S. E. Harris (New York: Knopf, 1947), 69–70 (emphasis added).
60. Keynes, *The General Theory*, 228.
61. In terms of Keynes's elucidation of the marginal efficiency of capital, we would simply expect present replacement costs in terms of money to fall relative to the net present value of future returns in terms of money. Real relative prices being unchanged, there should thus be no reason why an investment project that was previously viable at full employment should subsequently be rendered unprofitable merely because the value of money has risen.
62. Keynes notes that the stability feature is actually intricately bound up with the "essential" properties of money: "The expectation of relative stability in the future money-cost of output might not be entertained with much confidence if the standard of value were a commodity with a high elasticity of production. Moreover, the low carrying-costs of money as we know it play quite as large a part as a high liquidity-premium in making the money-rate of interest the significant rate." Keynes, *The General Theory*, 237.
63. See H. Townshend, "Liquidity-Premium and the Theory of Value," *Economic Journal* 47 (1937): 157–169.
64. Keynes, *General Theory*, 239.
65. On the question of nominal wage rigidities, Leijonhufvud concurs that there is no reason nominal wages should *not* be sticky. Workers "know (i) what they earned yesterday; (ii) that their physical productivity is unimpaired today; and possibly (iii) that the money stock has not decreased." While it is true "that their value productivity in terms of future goods has gone down—since we postulate a decline in MEC— . . . *if* the interest rate falls correspondingly (as it should) their discounted marginal value product should be (roughly) the same." Leijonhufvud, "The Wicksell Connection," 166n.
66. In fact, the problem may be exacerbated by nominal price flexibility, since uncertainty as to money prices may force further rises in the liquidity premium of money. See Keynes, *General Theory*, 232–233; J. Caskey and S. Fazzari, "Aggregate Demand Contractions with Nominal Debt Commitments: Is Wage Flexibility Stabilizing?," *Economic Inquiry* 25 (1987): 583–597; J. B. DeLong and L. H. Summers, "Is Increasing Price Flexibility Stabilizing?," *Journal of Money, Credit and Banking* 21 (1986): 481–497.
67. Keynes, *The General Theory*, 55.
68. Elisabetta De Antoni, "The Auctioneerless Economics of Axel Leijonhufvud: The 'Dark Forces of Time and Ignorance' and the Coordination of Economic Activity," *Cambridge Journal of Economics* 30 (2006): 88.

69. Axel Leijonhufvud, *On Keynesian Economics and the Economics of Keynes: A Study in Monetary Theory* (New York: Oxford University Press, 1968), 56.
70. Keynes, *The General Theory*, 215 (emphasis added).
71. Ibid., 214–215.
72. Ibid., 215–216.
73. Leijonhufvud, "The Wicksell Connection," 175 (emphasis in original).
74. And, in fact, the speculative element may be most important, since a smooth adjustment to a fall in the marginal efficiency of capital will require not just that speculators do not speculate against a decline in the market rate of interest but in fact that they speculate in its favor. See Lawlor, *Economics of Keynes in Historical Context*, 297–298.

Chapter 5

Pure Theory of Capital

Returning to Hayek from *The General Theory* demands a marked shift of gears, requiring that we relax the tautological *ex post* saving-investment identity, demote liquidity preference, and reincorporate Austrian capital theory. Inflation-enforced (as opposed to income-enforced) saving, emasculated by *The General Theory,* also reasserts itself.

Hayekian theory post-1936, however, was by no means *Prices and Production* redux. The Sraffian assault had exposed critical theoretical flaws in Hayek's model, not least of which was its inability to consistently explain the upper turning point of the cycle. In essence, for the task of proving Hayek's account of the crisis, the vast arsenal of Austrian capital theory he deployed either deserted or failed him. More fundamentally, however, Hayek, like Keynes, failed both to define Wicksell's natural rate in a multiple commodity world and also to justify his claims on capital intensity and interest in light of Wicksell effects.

Here, we address each of these issues in turn, beginning with Hayek's attempt to ground Wicksell's natural rate in a general theoretical framework of commodity own-rates of interest, which Hayek dubbed "rates of increase of the product." Second, we examine Hayek's generalization of Sraffa's own-rates schema to incorporate investment. Specifically, we will see that Hayek, like Keynes, considered investment a composite process, such that a lower "marginal efficiency of capital"—what Hayek terms the "marginal value product of investment"—will correspond to greater investment not because it encourages a greater degree of capital intensity in production but rather because it renders certain investment processes, previously unprofitable, inframarginal.

We conclude, then, by revisiting Wicksell's cumulative process, armed with Hayek's revised own-rates framework. While Hayek acknowledges the validity of Keynes's analysis under certain conditions, his own theory demonstrates why it is that liquidity preference cannot determine the volume of real investment in all cases whatsoever, but rather why under conditions resembling full employment, an inflation-fed boom must ultimately be self-reversing. In this sense, Hayek and Keynes could be said to have merely been theorizing on opposite sides of the same, Wicksellian coin.

5.1. RATES OF INCREASE OF THE PRODUCT

Recall that in chapter 17 of *The General Theory,* Keynes elaborated his interpretation of Sraffa's commodity rates of interest, redubbing them "own-rates of interest," so as to construct an asset market equilibrium with multiple real rates of return. In chapter 12 of *Pure Theory of Capital,* Hayek effectively assigns himself the same task and arrives at the same result as Keynes.

The building block of Hayek's analysis in chapter 12, "Planning for a Constant Output Stream," is what he designates the "rate of increase of the product." Despite a terminological *legerdemain,* the theoretical framework Hayek erects around his "rate of increase of the product" is in fact exactly analogous to Keynes's own-rates, and not surprisingly, for both are artifacts of the Sraffa imbroglio (though we should be clear to note that Sraffa himself was not keen on Keynes's construal of the own-rates concept).[1] Hayek, like

Keynes, observes that so long as there are different rates of return that can be obtained by investing different units of input for a given period, it will be advantageous to effect the corresponding changes to the composition of inputs so as to go on increasing the total size of the associated output stream. "Hence," he notes, "the condition for maximising the total income stream ... is that this rate of increase of the product due to an extension of the investment period by a given interval shall be the same for all investments."[2]

This assertion may, at first glance, appear to commit the same logical fallacy that was originally exposed by Sraffa, namely, the notion that all "natural" rates of interest must tend toward equality. But Hayek had indeed, like Keynes, absorbed the lessons of the Sraffa exchange, and accordingly acknowledges that whereas the rate of increase of the *physical* amount of any one input invested at an earlier date and the *physical* amount of that same input obtained at a later date may, and indeed will, differ for any two commodities, "the value equivalents in terms of the 'numéraire' at the two dates must bear the same ratio to one another for all commodities." That is to say, considering any single commodity, defined in its own technical units, at two discrete dates, where the quantity available at the later date can be increased only at the expense of the quantity available at the earlier date, there will exist a definite quantitative rate of increase due to the investment of that commodity. This ratio, moreover, will undoubtedly differ among different commodities, *even in equilibrium*. "But," Hayek stresses, "it will still be true that, measured *in terms of any one commodity*, the rate of increase will have to be the same for all commodities."[3] In other words, the value equivalents of any two commodities in terms of some third commodity at the two dates considered must bear the same ratio to one another, even though, as Hayek is keen to point out, the actual numerical value of this ratio will vary depending upon which commodity among many is selected as numéraire.[4]

This elucidation, we should note, is precisely the same as Keynes's own-rates setup in chapter 17. Hayek's "rate of increase of the product" includes both the real rate of return embodied in Keynes's *q*, *c*, and *l* terms, as well as his value appreciation, *a*, term. What is more, "there is no way," Hayek concedes, in a nod to Sraffa and Keynes, "in which this multitude of different 'own-rates of interest' (as Mr. Keynes has called these rates of increase in terms of particular commodities) can be reduced to one single rate which has a stronger claim than any other to be regarded as *the* rate of productivity of investment."[5] Nor, for that matter, is the physical productivity of investment of any primary concern. Keynes, recall, had dismissed the marginal physical productivity of "capital" as "insoluble and unnecessary."[6] Hayek, in *Pure Theory*, likewise notes that distinguishing that part of the rate of productivity of investment "due to circumstances affecting the value of the particular commodity and the part which is due to the productivity of investment is just as impossible as to divide the change in the relative value of two commodities." Thus, while "the search for this philosopher's stone is probably still being pursued by some economists," he concludes, "nothing more need be said about it here."[7] Wicksell's dilemma of accounting for possible changes in the value of every commodity relative to all other commodities is thus resolved in Hayek's and Keynes's second iterations of the Wicksell connection alike.

5.2. MARGINAL VALUE PRODUCT OF INVESTMENT

The own-rates method, however, while it relieves Hayek of the Sraffian critique, does not in and of itself resolve the question of the natural rate; that a set of *n* commodities traded over *m* time periods yields $n \cdot m$ commodity rates of interest that must, in equilibrium, be equal in terms of some arbitrarily chosen numéraire adds little clarity to Wicksell's natural–money rate mechanism. In other words, from which "natural" rate is the money rate free to diverge?

In *Prices and Production,* as in Wicksell's *Interest and Prices,* that rate was $\partial Q_{Value}/\partial K_{Value}$, namely, the marginal value product of homogeneous value capital expressed as an aggregate period of waiting—Böhm-Bawerk's average period of production. By *Pure Theory of Capital,* however, Hayek has jettisoned the average period entirely, denying both the validity of such a construction and its usefulness.[8] The fundamental complication is that in order to arrive at an aggregate figure of the amount of waiting involved in a production process, we have to assign definite weights to the different units of input, and these weights must necessarily be expressed in terms of value. But the relative values of the different kinds of input will inevitably depend on the rate of interest, so that such an aggregate cannot be regarded as something that is independent of, or as a datum determining, the rate of interest.[9]

This observation is obviously not new; Wicksell, as we have already seen, ascertained the same dilemma.[10] But whereas Wicksell nonetheless opted to retain the average period as a potentially useful mathematical concept, Hayek definitively and categorically rejects it.[11] According to Hayek, the fact that the amount of "waiting" involved in a particular production process is not simply proportional to the value of invested input, but rather dependent also on the interest rate, means that comparing any two investment projects, it will not generally be possible to determine, on strictly technical grounds, which involves the greater amount of waiting.[12] With multiple inputs and different technical combinations of inputs, it is possible that at one set of relative input prices (including interest), one combination of inputs will represent the greater degree of "waiting," while at another set of relative prices, another will.

The point will resonate with anyone familiar with the "Cambridge capital controversies" of the 1960s. To borrow the language of that later (and last) great controversy in capital theory, the circular dependence of the rate of interest on the value of the capital stock means that the rate of interest is determined not only by the exogenous technical properties of diminishing marginal productivity but also by endogenous relative prices, and this dependence complicates a Neoclassical value theory based on (price-independent) utility and relative scarcity. In other words, in standard Neoclassical value theory, as a commodity becomes physically scarcer, its relative price increases, and so too as its utility increases. Neoclassical capital theory is then merely the extension of this theory of value to production; the price of capital—that is, the rate of interest—is determined by the scarcity of capital relative to other factors of production, along with the technical productivity of capital. Neoclassical value theory thus gives rise to what Samuelson dubbed the three key "parables" of capital theory:

1. There is an inverse, monotonic relation between the quantity of capital and the rate of interest. That is, each incremental increase in the quantity of capital yields a lower marginal product, and thus a lower rate of interest.
2. The technical properties of the diminishing marginal product of capital determine, analogously to the diminishing marginal product of labor and the wage rate, the real rate of return on capital (i.e. the rate of interest).
3. The distribution of income between capital and labor is explained by their relative scarcities and marginal products.[13]

In essence, the marginal product of capital, $\partial Q/\partial K$, is a derivative of a physical quantity of output with respect to an incremental change in a quantity of capital, measured independently of relative prices, analogously to the marginal products of land (rent) and labor (wage rate). There is a one-directional chain of causation, from factor scarcities and the technical properties of production to relative factor prices, with changes in factor quantities causing inverse changes in factor prices.[14]

As we suggested in chapter 3, the implications of Wicksell effects for these three Neoclassical parables are not entirely innocuous. An illustration may be helpful in elucidating this point. Consider, for example, two production processes, *A* and *B*, as shown in figure 5.2.1. Both techniques produce one unit of output, using two inputs, labor and time. The combinations of these inputs differ, however, between the two techniques. In technique *A*, seven units of labor are invested for two periods, while in technique *B*, we have two units of labor invested for three periods, and six units invested for one period. Which technique is more capital-intensive? The answer depends on the rate of interest. At very high rates of interest ($r \geq 100\%$), the discount effect of compound interest on the two units of labor invested for three periods in technique *B* is massive, meaning technique *A* will be the cost-minimizing technique. At intermediate rates of interest ($100 \geq r \geq 50$), technique *A* becomes more expensive, hence technique *B* is chosen. But then at very low rates of interest ($r \leq 50$), the impact of interest is negligible, meaning labor is the decisive cost factor. In this case, technique *A*, with only seven units of labor in total, compared with eight in technique *B*, is again adopted.[15] The curve relating capital intensity to the rate of interest is thus not smooth, as shown in figure 5.2.2.

This "reswitching" phenomenon is essentially a wrong-signed real Wicksell effect, referring to a situation in which the same production technique (by which we mean the same capital-labor ratio) is cost minimizing at two or more rates of interest, while another or other techniques are cost minimizing at intermediate rates. Thus, as

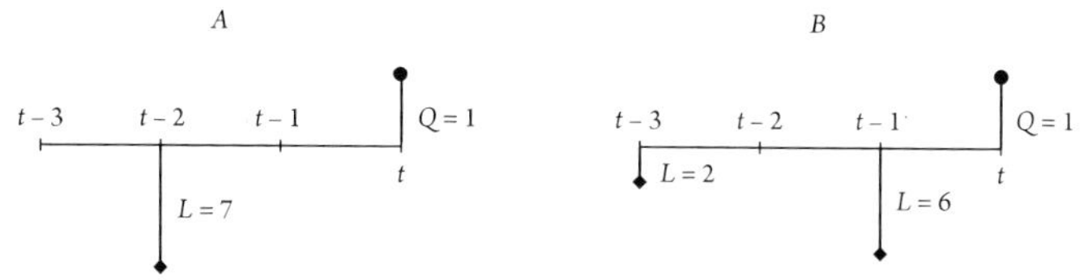

Figure 5.2.1

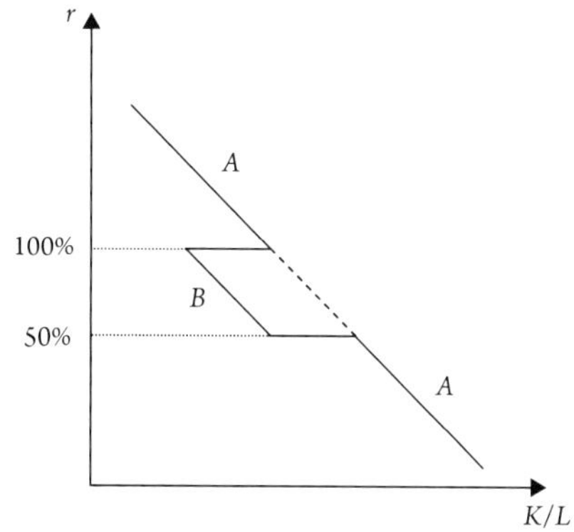

Figure 5.2.2

the interest rate falls, the cost-minimizing technique switches from *A* to *B*, but then "re-switches" back to *A* as the interest rate falls further, violating the second and third parables. A related perversity is "capital-reversing," meaning a wrong-signed price Wicksell effect. That is, with capital-reversing, a lower capital valuation obtains at a lower rate of interest. It is, therefore, as if the price of capital is decreasing with scarcity, implying a non-downward-sloping demand curve for capital, thereby violating the first and second parables.[16] The consequence is that we must evacuate our defense of correctly and unambiguously signed price effects of relative scarcity.[17]

Reswitching and capital-reversing represent something of a detour, albeit a necessary one, from our main discussion.

It is necessary inasmuch as Austrian capital theory—Böhm-Bawerk's capital theory—falls victim to the Cambridge critique. The problem is that with wrong-signed Wicksell effects, there is simply no way to aggregate capital into some "average period of production," the magnitude of which varies inversely with the rate of interest. The two-step process of determining first the quantity of capital and second the "price" poses an Escher-esque dilemma. Any theory of business cycle fluctuations that relies upon unambiguously signed oscillations between such an aggregate measure of capital intensity and the interest rate rests thus upon exceedingly fragile theoretical foundations. Hayek has consequently been often, and mistakenly, dismissed as simply another Austrian to be misled by Böhm-Bawerk's siren song, bogged down in a quagmire of problems pertaining to the measurement and aggregation of capital.

At the end of the day, however, if Hayek is to be rejected or dismissed, it ought not to be—indeed, cannot be—on the grounds that his theory falls victim to the Cambridge critique of Austrian capital theory. Though he no doubt made extensive use of the "average period" concept in *Prices and Production,* the exchange with Sraffa forced Hayek to closely scrutinize, and ultimately reject, the validity of any sort of average period of waiting. Indeed, by *Pure Theory,* he would assert that "there is no way in which the variety of technical periods during which we have to wait, either for the products of different kinds of input or for particular units of the product, can be combined into an aggregate or average which can be regarded as a technical datum."[18] Regardless of the procedure employed, the endogeneity of prices, including the interest rate, means not only that production techniques of differing lengths may alternately constitute the greater amounts of capital, depending on prevailing relative prices, but also that two techniques with the same average investment period may correspond to different quantities of capital, or amounts of waiting. "It is therefore," Hayek reiterates, "impossible to regard the average or aggregate investment period as a datum from which we can derive the marginal productivity of investment in the same manner as we determine the marginal productivity of any other factor of which there is a given quantity available."[19] His conclusion echoes an exasperated Keynes, who exclaimed to Dennis Robertson in 1935, "God knows what the Austrians mean by 'period of production.'"[20]

Hayek also, for that matter, echoes Wicksell, though he clearly goes far beyond Wicksell in rejecting the average period. In words that seem almost scripted for the Cambridge critics of Neoclassical capital theory, he declares up front that "attempts to explain interest, by analogy with wages and rent, as the price of the services of some definitely given 'factor' of production have nearly always led to a tendency to regard capital as a homogeneous substance the 'quantity' of which could be regarded as a 'datum,' and which once it had been properly defined, could be substituted, for the purpose of economic analysis, for the fuller description of the concrete elements of which it consisted."[21]

And nor was Hayek's a mere recognition of a potential problem. In discussing the difficulties with the average period of production concept, he in fact anticipates Samuelson's arithmetic illustration quite precisely, noting:

> The total length of time which elapses between the very beginning of the process and the completion of the product may be shorter in one process than in another, and yet by far the greater part of the input used may be applied very early in the first process and very late in the second process. Which of these two processes is to be regarded as the longer? It is impossible to answer this question at the present stage, and there is in fact no general answer to it.[22]

Perhaps more important, though, Hayek added that the issue was not only insoluble but irrelevant. The bitter and protracted capital controversies of the 1960s and 1970s between Cambridge, England, and Cambridge, Massachusetts (as well as, for that matter, the habit of previous and subsequent Austrian economists to get bogged down in intractable issues of measuring capital), would seem thus to constitute a regrettable detour. According to Hayek, the problem of capital measurement was, as it were, a red herring. All that need concern us is not "whether a whole process as such is longer or shorter than another," but rather only "the periods for which units of input are invested, and, secondly the fact that they will not be invested for longer periods unless the return due to them will be greater in consequence."[23] The abundantly evident repetition of this point is, we should stress, Hayek's, not ours; his disinheritance of Böhm-Bawerk's average period was clearly a stance on which he wished there to be no doubt or ambiguity.[24]

If we are to jettison the average period, however, Wicksell's natural rate of interest must be sought elsewhere. Hayek, like Keynes, turns to investment. That is, he recognizes that uniformity of own-rates of return (his "rates of increase of the product") must apply not only to individual commodities but also to composites of commodities. The fundamental point here is that for every investment process, all inputs "must be invested in such a way that the ratio between the marginal rate of increase of the product and the size of the whole product is the same for all units of input."[25] In other words, the increased value output attributable to extending the investment period of any particular unit of input within an investment process, expressed as a time rate and in terms of some numéraire, must be the same for all inputs involved in that process. If this were not the case, and the same value output could be obtained by investing one input for a shorter period and another for a slightly longer period, or else by investing more or fewer units of one input at any particular point in the production process, then the situation would not be one of equilibrium.[26]

Equilibrium, therefore, will obtain only when the discounted value of the total output stream resulting from an investment process is equal to the total value of the input invested in it.[27] And in order that this equivalence holds, "It must be possible to exhaust the total value of the output stream by allotting to each small unit of input a segment of the output stream such that the discounted value of that segment is equal to the value of the unit of input."[28] If the product is not so exhausted, and rather the discounted value of the output stream of any single investment process exceeds the value of the input invested in it, then it must be the case that particular inputs are yielding more in some investment processes than in others, in which case an arbitrage opportunity will exist to either invest more of those inputs in the process in which their rate of increase of the product is higher, or else to vary the period of time for which the inputs are invested in that process.[29] And, as any lengthening of the investment periods of particular inputs will necessarily reduce the output stream of those inputs maturing at an earlier date, thereby raising the relative value of that earlier output, the lengthening of certain investment periods will be accompanied by a shortening of the investment periods of other inputs, until it is the case that the product of the various units of input each matures "at such a rate that the value of the input whose product matures during any interval, plus compound interest for the period for which it has been invested, will be equal to the given value of the output stream during that interval."[30] Then, and only then, will there exist a uniform rate of return, in value terms, on investment. This uniform rate Hayek terms "the marginal value product of investment."

We should note that this is a different solution to the problem of capital from the "metastatic" approach of a Ramsey-Cass-Koopmans, overlapping generations (OLG), or von Neumann–type model, though it bears some passing resemblance. For von Neumann, input and output matrices collapse all processes into sequences of one-period activities of equivalent length, each producing intermediate goods.[31] Cass-Koopmans or OLG growth models essentially extend Fisher's two-period intertemporal transformation and substitution possibilities to an Arrow-Debreu-style general intertemporal equilibrium. That is, at root they suppose an economy of n commodities, with capital goods constituting distinct commodities (the outputs of previous periods), and so too the same commodities available at different dates. Thus, with T time periods, we have an nT-dimensional system, or, in the case of state-contingent commodities, with s different possible states, a total of nTs markets (with an Arrow security, $(n + s)T$ markets). Given standard assumptions of convexity and continuity, a solution to the system is determined, and that solution defines an efficient time path of consumption.[32] Though there will be neither a single own-rate for all commodities between any two periods nor a smooth, monotonically increasing rate for the same commodity over multiple periods, this is inconsequential; as Wicksell realized early on, there is no commitment on the part of general intertemporal equilibrium to the Neoclassical capital parables.[33] An interest rate is simply another exchange ratio that is reckoned, like all other prices, at $t = 0$, and hence need not detain our interest to a greater extent than any other price.

The idea of a rate of return on investment is thus extraneous; the system yields an equilibrium vector of prices, representing exchange ratios between different commodities, and between the same commodities in different time periods, which satisfies Walras's law. Though there will consequently be any number of own-rates of interest, which could each conceivably be expressed in terms of some randomly chosen commodity serving as numéraire, we have no more use of a composite of these own-rates than we would some composite of exchange ratios in a single period t. But this analytical correspondence of exchange ratios between different commodities and between the same commodities in different time periods (and contingent states) implies a deeper disagreement with Hayek, namely, that it holds time in suspense. It is, after all, the very nature of a system of simultaneous equations which requires that all markets, including all future contingent markets, be resolved at once. OLG or infinite-horizon models of optimal intertemporal consumption choice are practically inescapable, and once we are so committed, the trivial solution to the paradox of having to reconcile all choices before any choice can be made is to assume rational expectations—future contingent prices can be stochastically determined by all agents as simply the probability distributions of future prices consistent with the realization of optimal plans.[34] Time, therefore, is effectively collapsed into $t = 0$, and even a sequential analysis constitutes little more than the delivery of previously contracted goods, the exchange of goods (or Arrow securities for goods) at probabilistically predicted prices, or else recontracting at new market-clearing prices.

Hayek packs an immense degree of complexity into his equilibrium framework, such that it is easy to lose the forest through the trees. He is, after all, attempting to account both for heterogeneity among capital goods and for the element of time, such that we are asked to conceive of many different inputs participating in many different investment processes, all of the most theoretically thorny continuous-input—continuous-output variety. In spite of this complexity, however, it is important to spot that what Hayek is really describing is not simply a set of intertemporal rates of substitution but rather the marginal efficiency of capital. He is, moreover, no longer speaking in fundamentalist Austrian terms about the marginal product of a homogeneous fund of waiting known collectively as "capital" but instead opts for the same approach adopted by Keynes, namely, to consider the discount rate, δ_i, which will just bring the expected flow of returns net of costs of a particular investment project into line with its cost of production. Hayek's "marginal value product of investment," like Keynes's marginal efficiency of capital, is thus a composite concept, incorporating not merely static conditions but also expectations of continuous change: how relative prices may react (i.e., further elaborating the changes concealed by Keynes's a_i terms), techniques evolve, tastes and preferences change, and, most important, how the existence or absence of complementary investments may disappoint and compel the revision of production plans.[35]

This last point is worth dwelling on. For Hayek was certainly utilizing the notion of general equilibrium in an intertemporal setting, so it is tempting to mistake the meaning and purpose of the equilibrium concept in *Pure Theory of Capital*. The difference, with respect to the Walrasian system, is the difference between statics and dynamics. The problem of "capital," Hayek contends, arises once we contemplate how a stationary equilibrium might ever come about, or what the reaction of a given equilibrium to *unforeseen* change might be.[36] "Dynamics," he explains, "refers to an explanation of the economic process as it proceeds in time, an explanation in terms of causation that must necessarily be treated as a chain of historical sequences." What we then discover "is not mutual interdependence between all phenomena but a unilateral dependence of the succeeding event on the preceding one. This kind of causal explanation of the process in time is of course the ultimate goal of all economic analysis, and equilibrium analysis is significant only insofar as it is preparatory to this main task."[37]

The essential question, then, is not what the optimal allocation of resources will be, assuming that all individual plans mesh, but rather "whether the plans of different individuals *will* tally and will accordingly all stand a chance of being successful, or whether the present situation carries the seed of inevitable disappointment to some, which will make it necessary for them to change their plans."[38] That is, given their current state of knowledge, will entrepreneurs be able to execute the plans formed on the basis of that knowledge, or will they, in time, be required to revise those plans? And, in the event that observed outcomes do in fact depart from expectations, the question then becomes in which *direction* will the entrepreneur be impelled to revise his plans?[39]

Hayek's "marginal value product of investment" is, therefore, inherently inframarginal, describing an investment project that will be marginally viable *assuming* the existence of necessary cooperating investments. Or, as Hayek puts it, the success of any single investment process "will be dependent at each stage, not so much on the final demand as on the presence or absence of complementary instruments in proportionate quantities, and on there being people willing to use them in subsequent stages of production."[40] Considering, however, the fact that the entrepreneur can never know with certainty, or with certainty equivalent, the probability of these complementary investments obtaining in actuality, the equilibrium corresponding to any given marginal value product of investment is of a "purely fictitious character." That is, it does not refer to the rate of return prevailing at any actually observed terminal or stationary state, existing in the real world, but serves rather as a mere "preparatory" device for analyzing the correspondence or noncorrespondence between *ex ante* and *ex post* plans, where "equilibrium" defines the compatibility of individual plans *ex ante*. In this sense, Hayek's vision and use of the equilibrium construct bear greater resemblance to the interwar Swedish school descending from Wicksell, as well as to the temporary equilibrium approach embodied by the Hicksian "week," than to rational expectations or even Radner equilibrium analysis (though here, too, even the temporary equilibrium approach inflicts harm on dynamics, and Hayek did not withhold objections).[41]

Moreover, just as in Keynes's schema, the primary technical feature of the marginal value product of investment is not the property of diminishing marginal returns in purely physical terms but rather the effect of increased investment in any given production process on prices. Specifically, as more current resources are used "to remunerate input whose services are going to be invested,... the alternative current returns of this input will increase and, in addition, competition between the owners of the consumers' goods will drive up the prices of the resources of lower present productivity to a figure corresponding to its actual return discounted at the lower rate of interest now ruling."[42] In essence, if consumers' goods are to be diverted to alternative investment uses, "It will be necessary to pay a price higher than the (discounted) return from the shorter investment period."[43] Of course, the length of investment period is subject to Wicksell effects, but that is no longer relevant; the essential point is that insofar as the demand for the product of any investment project increases, the present supply price of that project, or more specifically the spot prices of the current goods entering into it, will be bid up. And, at the same time, the product attributable to this input will decline in value.[44] Adjustment to equilibrium, therefore, will proceed, as in Keynes's account, via either an increase in P_S^i or else lowered expectations of $\sum_{t=1}^{n} R_t^i$.

Considering the coincidence of Hayek's "marginal value product of investment" and what Abba Lerner redubbed Keynes's "marginal efficiency of investment," it should thus not be surprising that Hayek elects to construct a schedule relating the demand for investment to the rate of interest. This schedule, like Keynes's marginal efficiency of capital (or Lerner's equivalent marginal efficiency of investment) schedule, is *not* the orthodox marginal productivity of capital curve relating the rate of interest to capital intensity. As we have already noted, Hayek openly concedes that it is *impossible* to characterize different investment processes as "longer" or "shorter," and thus as more or less capital-intensive, in any unambiguous way, except, perhaps, in the *ex post* tautological sense of being adopted at a lower interest rate.[45,46] But it is nonetheless the case that a lower rate of interest means investment projects that would not otherwise be undertaken, either because the volume of their expected output functions was too small, or else the volume of the relevant input functions too large, will now be feasible. The rate of interest, then, determines "only to what point on the schedule investment will be carried," that is, it determines the last investment project that becomes economically viable.[47]

In this sense Hayek is in complete agreement with Keynes, who notes, in "Sundry Observations on the Nature of Capital" that "the ultimate quantity of *value* will not increase indefinitely... as the processes adopted become more and more roundabout, even if their physical efficiency is still increasing." That is, "only if the desire to postpone consumption" is strong enough will lengthy processes be adopted.[48] Hayek, likewise, notes that so long as there exist limits to the "amount of waiting for which people are prepared, processes that take more time will evidently not be adopted unless they yield a greater return than those that take less time."[49] Consequently, "we do not need to know whether a whole process as such is longer or shorter than another"; rather, the salient point is that specific inputs "will not be invested for longer periods unless the return due to them will be greater in consequence."[50] Keynes could hardly have disagreed.

5.3. THE CUMULATIVE PROCESS

In light of this shared emphasis on the salience of "waiting," it is instructive to recall Keynes's dinner analogy: if the consumer has decided to dine at eight o'clock, "it is the business of the cook to provide the best dinner he can for service at *that* hour." It matters not that he might be capable of producing a physically better, or bigger, dinner at a later hour (or earlier hour, for that matter). What matters is that he delivers the best meal he can, with the materials and time at his disposal, at eight o'clock. Thus, there is "a strict limit" to the proportion of prospective consumer demand that is profitable to provide for in advance.[51] But the impact that this time dimension of consumption will have on the relative prices of various types of capital goods is conveniently buried within Keynes's a_i terms.

As we have just seen, this calculus lies at the very heart of Hayek's analysis. His condition for equilibrium, after all, is that consumers and producers "must distribute their total resources between use for present and use for future consumption in such a way as to make the relative values of the different types of resources exactly proportional to their relative costs of production, where 'cost of production' includes the uniform time rate of return on resources invested."[52] While lengthening the period for which particular inputs are invested makes it *possible* to obtain a greater volume of output from a given volume of input, this output will mature at a later date than the smaller volume of output that might be obtained from a "shorter" process. The profitability of maintaining or altering the structure of production will depend, therefore, upon the discrepancy between the prices received for final output *at different dates,* and the cost of the corresponding input streams. Investment, per se, is only gainful if it delivers the *desired* quantity of output at the *desired* date, regardless of whether more output could be had at a different date.

Let us then resume the Wicksellian cumulative process with this proviso in mind. While Hayek, in *Pure Theory of Capital,* avoids use of the ambiguous term *natural rate,* the money–natural rate distinction remains nonetheless, in the form of Hayek's uniform time rate of return on investment, and the rate of interest on money loans. Moreover, the potential divergence of investment and saving resulting from a discrepancy between these two rates is not affected by Keynes's saving-investment identity, which Hayek, while not denying the fact that during any interval of time income not consumed must have been saved—and therefore, *ex definitione*, invested—considers an "irrelevant tautology."[53] Once again, a fall in the money rate of interest below the natural rate will, by lowering the rate at which an expected stream of net income can be discounted, serve as stimulus to investment. And, so long as there exist unemployed resources—that is, resources that can be newly called forth by investment *without* raising their price—then investment in all projects can proceed without forgone production of consumers' goods. In other words, investment demand will, as per Keynes's account, create its own savings via the multiplier, *not* via forced saving.[54]

But this scenario, in which every increase in investment demand can occur without any sacrifice of consumption, is, Hayek contends, possible only if we suppose the supply of all inputs to be infinitely elastic. While such a situation "may occasionally prevail in the depths of a depression," however, the assumption of "abundant unused reserves of all kinds of resources" is "certainly not a normal position on which a theory claiming general applicability could be based."[55] The "economics of abundance" upon which Keynes's multiplier relies are thus, in Hayek's view, of limited relevance.

Nor, though, does Hayek presume a situation of so-called full employment to be theoretically de rigueur. Rather, he assumes simply that in general, at any moment, while some, and perhaps even most, factors may be available in abundance, the presence of even a few definitely scarce factors must, through their effect on relative prices, impact the form that investment will take.[56] This effect of scarcity, moreover, will tend only to become more pronounced as investment demand increases, such that it cannot be the case that consumer-goods prices will remain indefinitely invariant.[57] The crucial question is thus when and in what manner will the influence of scarcity "reassert itself once this slack in the system has been taken up"?[58]

We must stress here that the money–natural rate gap *does not* inevitably imply greater capital intensity. Hayek, as we have seen, was keenly aware of Wicksell effects and thus rejected the average period—and, indeed, any attempt to reduce capital to a single measure of waiting—lock, stock, and barrel. He does not then attempt to smuggle the concept back in to his theoretical tool kit so as to analyze the cumulative process, and in fact explicitly forswears the claim that "any sacrifice of present income in order to increase future income (or the reverse) will necessarily lead to any net change in the amount of capital."[59] But while it is not valid therefore to speak in terms of definitive increases or decreases in capital intensity or, what is the same thing, "waiting," in response to a change in the rate of interest, it is legitimate to note that the rate of interest will have an effect on the *time distribution* of income. That is, we must "make a direct comparison of the intentions of the consumers and the intentions of the producers with regard to the *shape* of the income streams" they wish to consume and to produce, respectively.[60]

Specifically, we must consider how a lower rate of interest will affect the time rates of return on various types of input, assuming prices do not instantly and coordinately adjust to the increased supply of money. Since a lower interest rate means producers can discount expected returns over costs at a lower rate, inputs more closely associated with producing final output will evidently now earn a higher time rate of return than previously where they are invested for longer, as opposed to shorter, periods. Inasmuch as full-employment conditions prevent more of these inputs being invested in the same capital structure, in order to equalize time rates of return they will tend now to be invested for longer periods. That is, they will be invested in such a way that they yield final output at a later date than before the decline in the rate of interest.

Conversely, those inputs farther removed from the production of final output will, at the lower rate of interest, earn a higher time rate of return where they are invested for shorter duration, meaning equalization of rates of increase of the product will require that these inputs be now invested for shorter periods. The sum effect, therefore, is that while the direction of change in the *aggregate* "length" or period of waiting of the entire capital stock is indeterminate (and irrelevant), the gestation periods of the constituent inputs will be revised in such a way that final output will emerge at a later date than before the fall in the money rate.[61]

Such a realignment of the structure of production would be sustainable, though, only if the corresponding output profile were justified by the time preferences of consumers. All that has happened, however, is that the price of future income, in terms of present income, has been artificially "raised out of correspondence with the valuations of the consumers," meaning "consumers will find themselves getting less current real income, and consequently will attach a greater value to it compared with the sources of future income" (we are back to Keynes's dinner analogy).[62] In other words, the stream of money income remunerated to consumers on account of increased investment—factor incomes, after all, will have been driven up so as to lower the rate of increase of the product attributable to each input—will be meeting a diminished stream of consumer-good output. And, since saving preferences have not changed—consumers have not opted to restrict their current consumption—this *must* therefore mean higher money expenditure on consumer goods. In conditions even remotely resembling full employment, unless 100 percent of the additional income is saved, consumer-goods prices will inevitably rise relative to the various kinds of input.[63]

A rise in the relative price of final output will not, however, leave the optimal combination of various inputs unaffected. For although a given rise in the price of all output would, of course, increase the difference between the price of any unit of input producing a given marginal product and the price of that marginal product by the same amount, it would clearly change the *time rate* of profit earned on different units of input to very different degrees according to the periods for which the different units of input were invested.[64] This is a key distinction. By focusing attention on the rate of profit, rather than the rate of interest, Hayek avoids both the complications of the aggregate supply-of-savings/demand-for-investment formulation of the theory of interest—which gives rise to Wicksell effects—and the added difficulty that, at least in the short run, the interest rate may be guided first and foremost by speculative forces, and may thus serve as an imperfect mechanism of intertemporal coordination. Indeed, it is precisely because entrepreneurs must operate under conditions of uncertainty with respect to future prices that Hayek contends that in a dynamic, as opposed to metastatic, context, they will tend to be guided at least in part by profit margins and rates of turnover.[65] That is, in order that internal rates of return are equalized across firms, and across capital investments within a single firm, entrepreneurs will shift resources among production processes of higher or lower profit margins and corresponding lower or higher rates of turnover, according to the price signals conveyed by final demand. Consequently, it is not necessarily valid to assume that final demand and the yield on capital goods will always be positively correlated; demand for consumer goods and investment demand may move inversely. In fact, For Hayek, the assertion of this inverse movement is exactly what comprises the upper turning point of an inflationary boom.

For example, with a uniform internal rate of return of 6 percent per annum, a unit of input invested only one month before the completion of its product must earn a profit margin of 0.5 percent, while a unit of input invested two years before the completion of the product will require a profit margin of 12 percent.[66] But if the price of the final product rises by, say, 5 percent, then the input invested for only one month will now obtain a profit margin of 2.5 percent, for a per annum rate of 30 percent, while the input invested for two years will earn a profit margin of 14 percent, or only 7 percent per annum.[67]

Clearly, this represents a state of affairs that cannot be expected to persist. As Hayek notes, in the event that the difference between the price of a unit of input and the price of a unit of output rises, "a smaller marginal product maturing at a nearer date may well represent a higher time rate of profit... than the larger marginal product in the more distant future which, before the rise in the price of the product, promised the higher rate of return."[68] That is, any given increase in product prices relative to costs will enable producers to earn higher profits *per unit of time* on given inputs according as they are able to yield final output at an earlier date.[69] Hayek dubs this the "Ricardo effect."[70]

An illustration here may be helpful. Consider figure 5.3.1, with the total stock of fixed and circulating capital on the x-axis, and the total stream of current-period input on the y-axis.[71] Assume that, initially, receipts from total output, accruing at a time rate, are in the amount of $0F$. The profit-maximizing combination of capital stock and current input required to produce the given level of output will correspond to the point on the lower isoquant, A, tangent to a straight line drawn from F, as it is at this point that the ratio of profits (receipts, $0F$, minus current input, $0E$, or EF) to capital stock ($0C$) is maximized. Next, suppose a rise in the price of final product, such that receipts from output rise to F' from F. Isoquant A will now be tangent to the line drawn from F' at point P', which, as we can see, is above and to the left of P, meaning a higher ratio of profits ($E'F'$) to capital stock($0C'$), corresponding to both a larger volume of current input and a smaller capital stock. Thus, in this case in which the producer aims to produce a constant level of output, "though the total outlay in production will have increased, it will increase proportionally less than receipts," meaning a higher share of output for profits. Furthermore, "the distribution of current outlay between current cost of production and the maintenance of capital stock will also change: a larger proportion will go to the former and a smaller proportion to the latter." Hayek concedes that determining where to draw the line between "current costs" of output and "investment" in maintaining a given capital stock will inevitably be somewhat arbitrary, but he insists nonetheless that wherever we draw the line, the investment share of total receipts must fall and, with investment narrowly defined, so too must the absolute volume of investment. "The chief point," therefore, "that an increase in the demand for consumer goods will lead (in conditions of full employment) to a decrease in the demand for the kind of investment goods appropriate only to more highly capital-intensive methods of production, is thus established."[72] As we shall see,

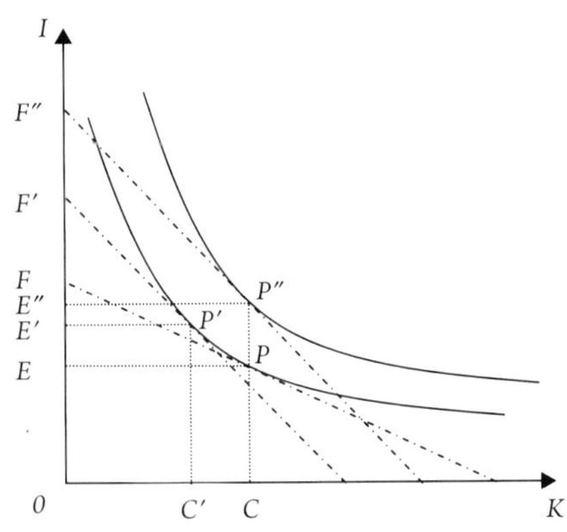

Figure 5.3.1 Credit: F. A. Hayek, "Three Elucidations of the Ricardo Effect," *Journal of Political Economy* 77 (1969): 276.

the full employment caveat is an essential one for understanding where Hayek parts company with Keynes.

Should the producer instead wish to raise production so as to maximize the return on the same amount of capital stock initially employed, the point at which that return is maximized will occur at point P'' along the higher isoquant A', corresponding to the same initial capital stock, C, but a higher level of receipts from output, OF''. P'' lies on the point of tangency between isoquant A' and the line drawn from OF'', which means that OE'' is the current input required to produce OF'', and that the ratio $E''F''/C$ will there be maximized by combining a larger volume of current input with a given capital stock.[73]

While the Keynesian response is that investment in all inputs and processes will be consequently scaled up until, either by diminishing marginal returns or by price pressures, the marginal efficiency of each investment is driven down to parity with the money rate, Hayek disagrees.[74] For although producers might succeed at times in driving input prices up to the discounted value of the *expected* price of their marginal product, "they could not possibly, whatever their effort," actually raise input prices to the figure corresponding to the lower rate of interest, "because the stuff to provide this income would just not be there."[75] In other words, as soon as higher factor incomes pass through to consumption, consumer prices will inevitably rise by proportionately *more* than the increase in money incomes. Channeling Wicksell, Hayek notes that "it is indeed the classical instance of a cumulative process," whereby the perfectly elastic supply of credit at a rate of interest below the "natural" rate "will be the cause of continuous changes of prices and money incomes where each change makes further changes necessary."[76]

For the fundamental point here is that what is provided is an infinite supply of money, not an infinite supply of productive factors. While there is no doubt that the former can indeed alter the price relationships "as determined by the 'real' factors" to a very considerable extent, the question is whether there exists no limit on the degree to which the real price structure can be so distorted, or whether instead the fact that the money which raises first one set of prices will eventually "work round" to affect the other set of prices (consumption goods) in the same direction imposes an upper bound to the extent of distortion.[77] The situation is rather, suggests Hayek, like pouring liquid into one side of a vessel, wherein "how far we shall be able to raise the level of one part above that of the rest will clearly depend on how fluid or viscid the liquid is." In no case "shall we be at liberty to raise the surface in one part of the vessel above the rest to any extent we like." Likewise, "The speed at which an increase of incomes leads to an increase in the demand for consumers' goods limits the extent to which, by spending more money on factors of production, we can raise their prices relative to those of the products."[78] Why, then, must the real variable, the natural rate, bear the full burden of adjustment to conform to a fixed nominal variable, the money rate of interest?

Hayek's answer is that it cannot. If investment depended solely on final demand, then we would have a situation in which every increase in consumer prices would lead to increased investment, which would in turn, at full employment, further reduce the supply of consumer goods relative to factor incomes. The process might then continue indefinitely, "presumably till there are no people left producing consumers' goods and everybody is engaged in providing machinery destined to produce consumers' goods in some distant future when the men will all have died of starvation in the interval."[79] That this result does not occur, Hayek contends, is, as we have seen, because investment of certain inputs for longer periods reduces the output stream at earlier dates attributable to these inputs, such that the value of output at these earlier dates is consequently raised.[80] Inputs that were, in response to the lower money rate of interest, invested for longer periods will now obtain a higher time rate of return by switching back to processes in which their output matures at an earlier date (regardless of whether those processes yield less output than longer ones). But inasmuch as certain of these inputs cannot readily be transferred to shorter production processes, their prices will rise and, in some cases, rise considerably.[81] Thus, while we might expect those other inputs that, on account of being farther removed from final output, were invested for shorter periods in response to the lower money rate to now earn a higher time rate of return if their investment periods are re-extended, this may not necessarily be the case; the rise in price among various nonspecific inputs will have squeezed margins in all processes not directly involved in final output.[82]

Nonetheless, Hayek's revised theory does *not* explain the economics of depression. In fact, as Hayek himself acknowledged, it claims to do nothing more than "account for the upper turning point of the typical nineteenth-century business cycle."[83] The "secondary deflation" to which he passingly referred in *Prices and Production* is given scant further attention in either *Pure Theory of Capital* or his numerous attempted elucidations of the Ricardo effect. Quite simply, Hayek's aim was to analyze the mechanism by which an inflation-fed boom must, sooner or later, be reversed by a decline in investment. "The cumulative process of contraction" likely to then set in, however, he wrote in 1969, "is another matter which must be analyzed by *conventional* means."[84] "Conventional means," in 1969, mean Keynesian means.

Indeed, as early as his 1942 article on the Ricardo effect, Hayek conceded (though his concession was buried in a footnote on the third page), "I am no longer so sure that the establishment of the truth of the proposition in the inverse form also proves the correctness of the original proposition."[85] That is, that the same mechanism which might arrest an inflation-fed boom should also reverse a deflation-led bust was no longer self-evident to him. After all, the cornerstone of Hayek's entire account of dynamic intertemporal equilibrium is the assumption that producers are guided in some degree by scarcity. If a cumulative contraction has already gotten under way, and the money rate rests above the natural rate, then it is no longer so clear how changing relative prices might overcome the expected fall in final demand. In this event, we have every reason to expect that, in the absence of immediate and *coordinated* nominal price adjustments, the multiplier effect will get under way.

There thus exists a theoretical asymmetry in Hayek's account of "Ricardo effect," in the sense that while his analysis offers a compelling case for why investment and final demand will be negatively correlated at the upper turning point of an inflation-fed boom, the inverse argument, that investment should increase in response to declining consumer demand, is less convincing.[86] In fact, one of the main ad hoc arguments Hayek introduces to support his contention that firms do not, in reality, face an infinitely elastic supply curve of credit that would allow them, in accordance with Neoclassical price theory, to scale up production without any change in their optimal input mix, actually cuts against him in the inverse case of declining consumer demand. As a practical matter, Hayek had argued, the more levered entrepreneurs become, the higher the risk premium they must be prepared to pay, which implies that the supply curve of credit facing the individual firm will have some slope to it, thereby reinforcing the shift away from higher margin, but lower turnover production processes as a boom proceeds.[87] But the reverse proposition that in the face of declining output prices efforts to drive internal rates of return up to parity with market rate of interest will eventually result in lower risk premiums, and thus a shift toward capital deepening, seems dubious at best. More likely, declining margins will raise, rather than lower, the risk premiums attached to investment loans, and thereby amplify, rather than counteract, any cumulative contraction underway. At this point, then, we must turn to the dynamics of liquidity- and/or income-constrained processes, a la Keynes.

Dennis Robertson and George Shackle would in fact later even go so far as to suggest that Keynes and Hayek were theorizing on opposite sides of the same, Wicksellian coin. Robertson suggested that Hayek's analysis explained the boom and turning point of an inflationary expansion, while Keynes's was necessary to understand the phenomenon of secondary deflation (which ensues from a crisis, the object of Hayek's theory).[88] In either case, both were fundamentally concerned with monetary *dynamics*. Shackle, in his foreword to the first English-language edition of Wicksell's *Value, Capital, and Rent* (1893), was explicit in highlighting the Wicksell connection between Hayek and Keynes. Referring to the "paradox" that two opposing theories could both invoke Wicksell's name, Shackle argued that "the flat contradiction in which the two theories seemed to confront each other was illusory; they were no more contradictory than the two statements, that if a stone is denser than water it will sink, and if a cork is less dense than water it will float."[89] That a former Hayek student turned post-Keynesian should appreciate the elements of concurrence between Hayek and Keynes should indeed be telling.

Hayek mentions Keynes by name in eleven distinct instances in *Pure Theory*. He refers to Keynes once on a technical point concerning the definition of durable goods, once to suggest that the *ex post* identity of saving and investment is not a particularly instructive device, and twice to object to what he calls Keynes's "economics of abundance." The remaining seven references to Keynes are all criticisms of the theory of liquidity preference. Here, it would seem that Hayek missed his mark. This is certainly not the place to rehash the interminable liquidity preference versus loanable funds debate.[90] It is nonetheless worth noting, however, that regardless of the merits or novelty of Keynes's theory of liquidity preference, Hayek deliberately chose to conduct his study in real terms and while operating on the assumption of full, or near-full, employment. But as he himself concedes, it is precisely when we admit the possibility of unemployed resources that the role of liquidity assumes central importance in understanding dynamics. Of this fact, Hayek was certainly aware, noting in six unique places in *Pure Theory* that the problems of monetary dynamics were outside the scope of his analysis, meriting a separate study unto themselves, for which *Pure Theory* was supposed to be merely preparatory.

Concerning this qualification, Hayek is quite explicit and, indeed, a tad tedious. He explains that "we must leave the consideration of the existence of unemployed resources of certain kinds to more specialised investigations of dynamic problems," and, again, that his concern is "not with the transitory effects which occur while any unused capacity caused by a previous slump is being absorbed—the analysis of this is the proper subject of dynamic studies—but with the way in which the influence of scarcity will reassert itself once this slack in the system has been taken up."[91] Recognizing, moreover, the complexity of the relationships between various rates of interest over periods of different lengths in a non-stationary economic system, he likewise acknowledges that the problem "belongs more to the field of monetary theory or economic dynamics generally than to the field of general equilibrium analysis to which this book has been mainly confined."[92] More succinctly, "A full treatment of the economic process as it proceeds in time, and of the monetary problems that are connected with this process, is outside the compass of this book."[93] Accordingly, transforming those elements of the "pure" theory of capital into a form which might "prove useful for the analysis of the monetary phenomena of the real world," is, he suggests, "important enough to merit a separate study."[94]

Hayek's repetition of the perimeter of his analysis renders his failure to recognize the different suppositional terrain of his and Keynes's theories quite surprising and, for that matter, unfortunate. Keynes freely admitted that in the event that aggregate output is at a level "corresponding to full employment as nearly as is practicable, the classical theory comes into its own again from this point onwards."[95] Analogously, Hayek appears to appreciate that outside of full or near-full employment, liquidity concerns become fundamental, if not decisive, in describing adjustment dynamics. His preoccupation, it seems, with Keynes's emphasis on liquidity preference stems from his objection to the generalization of liquidity preference to full-employment situations. If the economy is ever to effect a transition from one growth-theoretic state to another, the effective operation of relative price signals is essential.

Hayek never did get around to writing the second volume, of which *Pure Theory* was intended to be "preparatory." Even before the 1941 publication of *Pure Theory* (indeed, as early as his 1937 *Economica* article, "Economics and Knowledge"), Hayek's research—or rather, the angle from which he approached his research interests—had begun to pivot away from business cycle theory and capital theory proper, and toward questions concerning the coordination of economic activity in a world of dispersed knowledge. But already in *Pure Theory,* Hayek, like Keynes, observes that, "in a world of imperfect foresight, not only the size of the capital stock, but also the income derived from it, will inevitably be subject to unintended and unpredictable changes which depend on the extent and distribution of foresight."[96] The question, then, is whether and how plans that were improperly conceived might be revised in the "right" direction, and to what extent the final consistency of plans is in fact possible in a world in which prices fail, at times, to correctly communicate knowledge, and do so with adequate relative velocities.

As one of Hayek's students, Ludwig Lachmann, would later put it, "Dynamic equilibrium requires consistency of plans which, in its turn, depends on a flexible price system. Inconsistency of plans is an inevitable feature of a world in which prices (including forward prices and share prices) no longer tell an intelligible story."[97] But it is not just price *flexibility* that is at issue; it is also a matter of flexible prices conveying the *correct* signals—that is, a matter of accurately translating changes in conditions of supply and demand into corresponding changes in price, and vice versa.[98] When multiple simultaneous changes are transmitted via prices at varying velocities, however, it may, indeed, be "impossible to reconstruct the chronological order in which the events to which they give expression actually occurred," meaning expectations about future input and output streams will not be coincident. In this instance, structural maladjustment, or "inconsistent capital change," must result.[99] Inasmuch as money or any stocks of liquid assets permit trading at "false" prices for some nontrivial period of time, such inconsistent change may in fact be exacerbated, rather than attenuated, by flexible prices. Taking a cue from Keynes, Lachmann would even examine the potentially destabilizing role of speculators, whose attempts to anticipate in period t changes in period $t + 1$, rather than translate the messages of $t - 1$, will affect prices that others accept as data, "their point of orientation."[100] Hayek nevertheless insists that "monetary changes are bound to set up expectations which will inevitably be disappointed." Before they are, however, the real situation may be very considerably distorted, meaning money is bound also "to lead to constant fluctuations of economic activity."[101] But we must then ask, like Keynes, whether and to what extent these "very considerable" distortions may override the stabilizing forces at work and so act to deflect expectations from, rather than reflect them toward, what would be required for consistent and coordinated capital change. This, indeed, is the heart of the Wicksell connection.

NOTES

1. Heinz D. Kurz, "Keynes, Sraffa, and the Latter's 'Secret Skepticism,'" in *The Return to Keynes*, ed. Bradley W. Bateman, Toshiaki Hirai, and Maria Cristina Marcuzzo (Cambridge, MA: Harvard University Press, 2010), 184–204.
2. F. A. Hayek, *The Pure Theory of Capital* (1941; reprint, Chicago: University of Chicago Press, 1975), 165.
3. Ibid., 167–168 (emphasis added). For example, the percentage increase in wine output from allowing grapes to age for an additional month must equal, *in value terms*, the percentage increase in output from likewise extending any other production process by one month, holding pure input constant.
4. Ibid., 167, 243–244. Put differently, for a commodity that is increasing in relative value per unit, in order that the percentage return to investment in that commodity versus any other commodity is equal in value terms, the percentage growth in physical units of this particular commodity must be less than that of commodities that are decreasing in relative value per unit. Consider, for instance, two commodities, x_1 and x_2. If x_2 is expected to appreciate, from one date to another, relative to x_1, that means at the second date a smaller quantity of x_2 trades for a given quantity of x_1. With x_1 as numéraire, equilibrium would then demand that the rate of interest in terms of x_2 be smaller than the rate in terms of x_1. The same would apply, mutatis mutandis, if x_2 were expected to fall in value relative to x_1.
5. Ibid., 168–169 (emphasis in original).
6. J. M. Keynes, *The General Theory of Employment, Interest and Money* (1936; reprint, Cambridge: Cambridge University Press, 1973), 138.
7. Ibid.; Hayek, *Pure Theory*, 172.
8. Hayek was somewhat reluctant to surrender the average period of production. While he acknowledged as early as 1934 that the average period depended upon the rate of interest, and thus could not be regarded as a "technical datum," it was not until 1936 that he conceded "full sympathy with those who see in the concept of a single or average period of production a meaningless abstraction which has little if any relationship to anything in the real world." F. A. Hayek, "On the Relationship between Investment and Output," *Economic Journal* 44 (1934): 227; F. A. Hayek, "The Mythology of Capital," *Quarterly Journal of*

Economics 50 (1936): 200. For more on Hayek's protracted debate on Austrian capital theory with Frank Knight, see Avi Cohen, "The Hayek/Knight Capital Controversy: The Irrelevance of Roundaboutness, or Purging Processes in Time?," *History of Political Economy* 35 (2003): 469–490; Avi Cohen, "Frank Knight's Position on Capital and Interest: Foundation of the Hayek/Knight/Kaldor Debate," in *The Economic Mind in America: Essays in the History of American Economics*, ed. M. Rutherford (London: Routledge, 1998).

9. Hayek, *Pure Theory*, 143.
10. Knut Wicksell, *Lectures on Political Economy*, vol. 1, *General Theory*, ed. Lionel Robbins, trans. E. Classen (1901; reprint, London: Routledge and Kegan Paul, 1935), 184.
11. Hayek credited Wicksell for recognizing that the value of capital, as well as the period of production, are not data but rather among the unknowns to be determined simultaneously with the relative values of the system. He criticized Wicksell, however, for his failure to "consistently follow this up," suggesting that Wicksell "discovered this point rather late and never fully incorporated it in his system." Hayek, *Pure Theory*, 192. See also Wicksell, *Lectures*, 1:202.
12. Hayek, *Pure Theory*, 144.
13. See Avi J. Cohen and G. C. Harcourt, "Retrospectives: Whatever Happened to the Cambridge Capital Theory Controversies?," *Journal of Economic Perspectives* 17 (2003): 199–214; Avi Cohen and G. C. Harcourt, "Introduction: Capital Theory Controversy: Scarcity, Production, Equilibrium and Time," in *Capital Theory*, ed. Christopher Bliss, Avi J. Cohen, and G. C. Harcourt, vol. 1 (Cheltenham: Edward Elgar, 2005), xxvii–lx.
14. Cohen and Harcourt, "Retrospectives," 201; Cohen and Harcourt, "Introduction," xxxi.
15. This example was actually devised during the Cambridge capital controversies. The production profiles are obviously very simple, and the interest rate values extreme, but they were selected for the purpose of illustrating the point while keeping the arithmetic simple. Far from being an anomaly, the example above may actually represent the more general case. See Paul Samuelson, "A Summing Up," *Quarterly Journal of Economics* 80 (1966): 568–583.
16. See Cohen and Harcourt, "Retrospectives," 202.
17. Ibid. See also Cohen and Harcourt, "Introduction," xxxii.
18. Hayek, *Pure Theory*, 145.
19. Ibid., 190. See also 76, 145, 190–192, 199–200.
20. Keynes to Robertson, February 20, 1935, in *The Collected Writings of John Maynard Keynes*, ed. Donald Moggridge, vol. 13, The *General Theory and After, Part I: Preparation* (London: Macmillan, 1973), 517.
21. Hayek, *Pure Theory*, 5.

22. Ibid., 76.
23. Ibid.
24. Consider again: "All attempts to reduce the complex structure of waiting periods, which is described by the input functions *and* the output functions, to a single aggregate or average investment period, which could be generally substituted for these functions in the discussion of the productivity of investment, are bound to fail, because the different waiting periods cannot be reduced to a common denominator in purely technical terms." Hayek, *Pure Theory*, 141–142 (emphasis in original).
25. Ibid., 191.
26. Ibid., 179, 181–182.
27. Ibid., 214.
28. Ibid., 209.
29. Ibid., 204–205.
30. Ibid., 190–191, 209.
31. J. von Neumann, "A Model of General Economic Equilibrium," *Review of Economic Studies* 13 (1945–1946): 1–9; F. P. Ramsey, "A Mathematical Theory of Saving," *Economic Journal* 38 (1928): 543–559; David Cass, "Optimum Growth in an Aggregative Model of Capital Accumulation," *Review of Economic Studies* 32 (1965): 233–240; Tjalling C. Koopmans, "On the Concept of Optimal Economic Growth," Cowles Foundation Discussion Papers 163, Cowles Foundation for Research in Economics, Yale University (1963). For the neo-Walrasian approach to the capital problem, see especially Christopher Bliss, *Capital Theory and the Distribution of Income* (Amsterdam: North-Holland, 1975); Edmond Malinvaud, "Capital Accumulation and Efficient Allocation of Resources," *Econometrica* 21 (1953): 233–268; Frank H. Hahn, "The Neo-Ricardians," *Cambridge Journal of Economics* 6 (1982): 353–374; Peter A. Diamond, "National Debt in a Neoclassical Growth Model," *American Economic Review* 55 (1965): 1126–1150.
32. Axel Leijonhufvud, *On Keynesian Economics and the Economics of Keynes* (New York: Oxford University Press, 1968), 224–225.
33. Frank H. Hahn, "General Equilibrium Theory," in *The Crisis in Economic Theory*, ed. D. Bell and I. Kristol (New York: Basic Books, 1981), 128.
34. Axel Leijonhufvud, "The Metamorphoses of Neoclassical Economics," in *Evolution of the Market Process: Austrian and Swedish Economics*, ed. Michel Bellet, Sandye Gloria-Palermo, and Abdallah Zouache (New York: Routledge, 2005), 5. See also Leijonhufvud, *On Keynesian Economics*, 224–230.
35. Hayek, *Pure Theory*, 166–167, 263–264, 332.
36. Ibid., 8.
37. Ibid., 17.
38. Ibid., 22 (emphasis added).
39. Ibid., 22–23.

40. Ibid., 25.
41. Ibid., 19–20, 23.
42. Ibid., 257–258.
43. Ibid., 258.
44. Ibid., 204–205.
45. Ibid., 76, 144–145. On the question of the tautology of "capital intensity," see also Samuelson, "Summing Up," 582–583.
46. Hayek further rejects the Neoclassical assumption that all increases in the capital-to-labor ratio must correspond to commodities being invested in "longer" processes than before: "So long as the processes used in different industries are of different lengths, this is by no means a necessary consequence." That is, "If input is transferred from industries using shorter processes to industries using longer processes, there will be no change in the length of the period of production in any industry, nor any change in the methods of production of any particular commodity, but merely an increase in the periods for which particular units of input are invested." Hayek, *Pure Theory*, 77–78.
47. Ibid., 389.
48. J. M. Keynes, *General Theory*, 214 (emphasis in original). The fact that Keynes even speaks in terms of "roundaboutness" is a testament to the lingering Wicksellian voice.
49. Hayek, *Pure Theory*, 73.
50. Ibid., 76.
51. Keynes, *General Theory*, 215–217.
52. Hayek, *Pure Theory*, 264.
53. Ibid., 394n–395n. Hayek further acknowledges that in a definitional sense saving and investment "are always equal, or are made equal by the pricing process." But the fact that two categories of expenditure may coincide is beside the point, since "the ultimate test for the correspondence between saving and investment in the relevant sense is really whether the current demand and the current supply of consumers' goods are so matched that there is no inducement either to increase or to decrease this current supply at the expense or in favour of the provision of the future." Ibid., 338, 341.
54. Ibid., 370–371.
55. Ibid., 373–374.
56. "What is relevant is not whether full employment exists, but whether the particular kinds of resources needed exist in the proportions corresponding to the state of demand." Ibid., 391.
57. Ibid., 376–377. For more on the role of scarcity in Hayek's version of Austrian capital theory, see Ludwig Lachmann, *Capital and Its Structure* (London: Bell and Sons, 1956), 100–127.
58. Hayek, *Pure Theory*, 377.

59. Ibid., 335.
60. Ibid., 337.
61. Ibid., 281–283, 337–341, 393.
62. Ibid., 339.
63. Ibid., 378–380. Hayek elaborates: "In such a situation no monetary change can alter the fact that relatively to every unit of input employed there is less output available, and that, therefore, unless people spontaneously decide to save correspondingly more, the price of input in terms of output must fall."
64. Ibid., 381–382.
65. See Fiona Cameron Maclachlan, *Keynes' General Theory of Interest: A Reconsideration* (London: Routledge, 1993), 146–152.
66. Disregarding compound interest for the sake of simplicity. For a more thorough explanation, see also F. A. Hayek, *Profits, Interest, and Investment* (London: George Routledge and Sons, 1939), 8; F. A. Hayek, "The Ricardo Effect," *Economica* 9 (1942): 132–133.
67. We can also think of this, as Hayek does in "The Ricardo Effect," in terms of "rate of turnover," that is, the number of times the amount expended on an input or investment process is received back as revenue in the course of a year. Defining the per annum percentage return (Hayek's time rate of return) as the "internal rate of return," I, and the profit margin, M, as the proportional gain on each turnover, we then have the relationship $I = TM$.

    From this relationship, it is easy to compute the effect of a rise in price margins on the internal rates of return of various inputs, depending upon the rate at which they are "turned over." For instance, if the price of product rises by 2 percent, then, holding input prices constant, there will be an addition to the profit margins earned on each turnover equal to the amount of the rise. The firm turning over its capital twice a year will find its profit margin increased from 3 to 5 percent, while that of the firm turning over its capital once a year will rise from 6 to 8 percent. Multiplying these profit margins by the corresponding rates of turnover, we obtain the new internal rates of return of 10 percent per annum for the former and 8 percent per annum for the latter. See Hayek, "The Ricardo Effect," 131–134. Hayek cites Kenneth Boulding for suggesting the term "internal rate of return." See K. E. Boulding, "The Theory of a Single Investment," *Quarterly Journal of Economics* 49 (1935): 478.
68. Hayek, *Pure Theory*, 384.
69. Hayek, "The Ricardo Effect," 132.
70. There was considerable controversy over this label. The proposition that Hayek attributes to Ricardo was that a rise in the wage rate would induce producers to substitute machinery for labor, since the machine must require fewer man-hours than its labor equivalent, otherwise it would not be built. Hayek considers the inverse proposition, namely, that a fall in the real wage

must induce a substitution of labor for labor-saving (i.e., machine) methods of production. For more on the Ricardo effect, see L. S. Moss and K. I. Vaughn, "Hayek's Ricardo Effect: A Second Look," *History of Political Economy* 18 (1986): 545–565; C. E. Ferguson, "The Specialization Gap: Barton, Ricardo, and Hollander," *History of Political Economy* 5 (1973): 1–13; M. Blaug, *Economic Theory in Retrospect*, 3d ed. (Cambridge: Cambridge University Press, 1978), 571–576.

71. This figure is reproduced from F. A. Hayek, "3 Elucidations of the Ricardo Effect," *Journal of Political Economy* 77 (1969): 276. Hayek assumes a linear and homogeneous production function for simplicity, though this assumption does not alter the resulting conclusions. He further notes that since the variables on both coordinates "consist of variable combinations of heterogeneous goods and services, these can of course be represented only in value terms," which "would be strictly legitimate only if we could assume that the prices of the various goods and services involved remain constant. In fact, however, the changes which we will consider necessarily involve some changes in the relation between these prices." He nonetheless contends that despite "the slightly unsatisfactory nature of this technique," the "defect is of comparatively minor significance and does not seriously detract from the validity of the conclusions which can be derived in a comparatively simple manner by these methods." Ibid., 275.
72. Ibid., 276.
73. Ibid., 275–277. Though here Hayek flirts dangerously with old-school Austrian language by arguing that "this unchanged total quantity of capital will again have to consist of less laborsaving or less durable equipment than before; the demand for the more laborsaving or more durable kinds of equipment will therefore fall."
74. For the Keynesian view of Hayek's proposition, see Nicholas Kaldor, "Capital Intensity and the Trade Cycle," *Economica* 6 (1939): 40–66; T. Wilson, "Capital Theory and the Trade Cycle," *Review of Economic Studies* 7 (1940): 169–179; Nicholas Kaldor, "Professor Hayek and the Concertina-Effect," *Economica* 9 (1942): 359–382.
75. Hayek, "The Ricardo Effect," 143. See also Hayek, *Pure Theory*, 383.
76. Hayek, "The Ricardo Effect," 141.
77. Ibid., 142.
78. Ibid.
79. Ibid., 144.
80. Hayek, *Pure Theory*, 190–191.
81. Ibid., 384–385. This will particularly be the case in those instances where the quantity available for the production of consumers' goods cannot in the short run be increased at all, but increased use of cooperating factors might nonetheless raise output. An example would be raw materials, the price of

which might often rise by proportionately *more* than the price of their final product during the later stages of a boom. For while the supply of raw materials available for consumer-goods production cannot, in the short run, be easily increased, more intense use of other factors that cooperate with raw materials in the production of consumer goods might nonetheless raise output of consumer goods, meaning the price of raw materials would have to rise by considerably more in order to close the gap to its now higher marginal product. Note that this concept is closely related to the idea of "nonspecific producers' goods" in *Prices and Production*.

82. Hayek describes this effect in terms of a "tilting" of the investment demand curve. Ibid., 386–387. See also Hayek, *Profits, Interest, and Investment*, 34.
83. Hayek, "3 Elucidations," 282.
84. Ibid. (emphasis added).
85. Hayek, "The Ricardo Effect," 129.
86. Machlachlan, *Keynes' General Theory of Interest*, 153.
87. Hayek, "3 Elucidations," 282–284.
88. D. H. Robertson, "Industrial Fluctuations and the Natural Rate of Interest," in *Essays in Monetary Theory* (London: P. S. King, 1940), 83–91. The Robertson link is pointed out by Gerald O'Driscoll; see Gerald P. O'Driscoll, *Economics as a Coordination Problem: The Contributions of Friedrich A. Hayek* Kansas City, MO: Sheed Andrews and McMeel, 1977), 73.
89. G. L. S. Shackle, foreword to *Value, Capital, and Rent*, by Knut Wicksell, trans. S. H. Frowein (1893; reprint, London: George Allen and Unwin, 1954), 7–8.
90. For a review of both the early and late debates over liquidity preference versus loanable funds, see Maclachlan, *Keynes' General Theory of Interest*, 102–125.
91. Hayek, *Pure Theory*, 376–377.
92. Ibid., 397.
93. Ibid., 4.
94. Ibid.
95. Keynes, *General Theory*, 378.
96. Hayek, *Pure Theory*, 335.
97. Lachmann, *Capital and Its Structure*, 116.
98. Ibid., 62.
99. Ibid., 63.
100. Ibid., 22.
101. Hayek, *Pure Theory*, 407.

Chapter 6

Keynes, Hayek, and the Wicksell Connection

As alluded at the start of this book, the two decades since New Keynesianism convincingly entered the economics lexicon have witnessed a striking convergence in macroeconomic modeling, with, in Olivier Blanchard's words, a macroeconomic article today often following "strict, haiku-like, rules."[1] The standard model consists of three equations: one for aggregate demand, derived from the first-order conditions of forward-looking utility maximization by consumers; a second for aggregate supply, derived from the first-order conditions of profit-maximizing firms; and, third, some form of Taylor rule to describe the response of interest rates to inflation and an output gap. Finally, price rigidity, typically in the form of monopolistic competition and staggered pricing (Calvo pricing is the most common choice), is appended to yield short-run deviations from full employment.

As Blanchard notes, this "workhorse" model has become "ubiquitous."[2] According to Varadarajan Chari, Patrick Kehoe, and Ellen McGrattan, "Macroeconomists have largely converged on method, model design, reduced-form shocks, and principles.... Our main disagreements are about implementing the methodology."[3] New Keynesian standard-bearer Michael Woodford agrees, suggesting that "in fact there are fewer fundamental disagreements among macroeconomists now than in past decades."[4] In Blanchard's words,

"The state of macro is good." By incorporating price rigidities into a coherent, Walrasian-style intertemporal general equilibrium system, the New Keynesian program has in effect checked all the right boxes.

Though the derivation of the standard New Keynesian model is somewhat tedious and highly technical, it need not detain us here. Ultimately, the model can be distilled into three simple equations. First, we have a forward-looking *IS* curve, reflecting optimal consumption by households. Since the standard model ignores investment, consumption demand is equivalent to aggregate demand and is a function of the interest rate and expected future consumption. The *IS* curve thus takes the form:

$$x_t = -\varphi\left(i_t - E_t \pi_{t+1}\right) + E_t \pi_{t+1} + \upsilon_t$$

where x_t is the output gap (the difference between current and potential or trend output, or what output would be in the absence of nominal rigidities), i_t the nominal interest rate, $i_t - E_t\pi_t$ the real interest rate, π_t the inflation rate, and υ_t a demand shock. The output gap is inversely related to the real interest rate owing to an intertemporal substitution effect—higher returns induce households to save more in the current period, which lowers current aggregate demand, and thus output. The output gap is also positively related to the expected future output gap, as households desire to smooth consumption over time; higher expected output in period $t + 1$ will therefore raise consumption demand in period t.

An aggregate supply curve assumes the form of a Phillips curve–like equation with Calvo-style monopolistic pricing (i.e., staggered price setting, which generates price "stickiness"), as follows:

$$\pi_t = \lambda x_t + \gamma E_t \pi_{t+1} + \mu_t$$

This New Keynesian Phillips curve, derived from the profit-maximizing price and output decisions of firms, thus gives inflation as a function of the output gap and expected future inflation, as well as random cost-push shocks (μ_t). Finally, a Taylor-style monetary policy rule constitutes the *LM* curve:

$$i_t = r_t + \theta_x E_t x_{t+1} + \theta_\pi E_t \pi_{t+1}$$

This is essentially a reaction function, relating the nominal interest rate chosen by the central bank to expected inflation and the expected output gap, so as to target a given real interest rate.

Putting together these three pieces of the New Keynesian model, let us then consider, as we did for Wicksell and Keynes, an adverse demand shock, as shown in figure 6.1.[5] Suppose we begin at full employment ($x_0 = 0$), with $LM_0 = IS_0$ and the (natural) rate of interest rate equal to r_0. The adverse demand shock corresponds to a downward shift of the *IS* curve, from IS_0 to IS_1, as shown in panel A, and a downward shift of aggregate demand, as shown in panel B. Since prices do not immediately adjust, we thus find ourselves at an interest rate such as r_1, with an output gap of $x_1 < 0$. As we can see in panel B, however, the aggregate demand curve now intersects the Phillips curve at a rate of inflation less than zero. The consequent deflationary pressure therefore leads to a gradual outward shift of the *LM* curve, in accordance with the Taylor rule specification. This outward shift gradually nudges aggregate demand back to its full-employment level, moving up along the Phillips curve. Once the output gap is thereby eliminated, there is no further deflationary pressure, and thus no further movement of the *LM* curve. In other words, in the long run, the economy returns to its "natural" level of output, namely, the level consistent with full price flexibility.

Note that the interest rate plays no more than a passive role in this process. The interest rate is neither the culprit nor the savior in

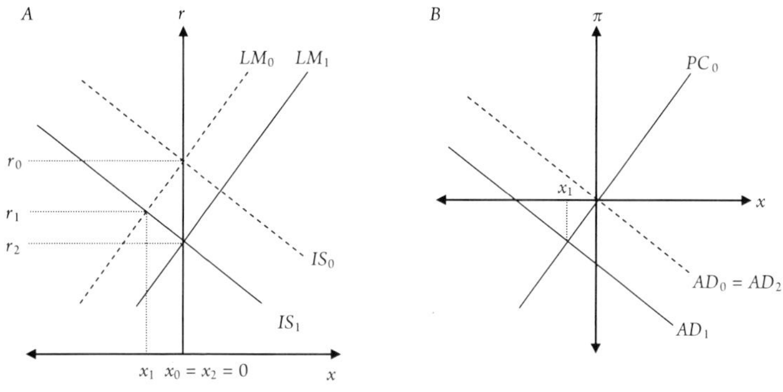

Figure 6.1

the sequence just described; it is the price level that is doing all the work in this model. To be sure, it is the fall in the real rate of interest, owing to the outward shift of the Taylor-based *LM* curve, which restores aggregate demand to its full-employment level. But this is not an autonomous fall; it is merely the consequence of price level adjustment. Indeed, if we want to trace the time path of the economy, it is to the New Keynesian Phillips curve, not planned saving and investment, that we must look. The challenge facing agents in the New Keynesian model is not finding the rate of interest that will coordinate intertemporal economic activity at full employment but rather in forecasting the rate of inflation. On this basis, the New Keynesians might consider themselves better off joining Lucas and the New Classicals rather than retaining the Keynesian label. In a sense, it is merely the Phillips curve debate—Neoclassical Keynesians versus monetarists—round two, but with substantially less acrimony.

The key point here is that in the Wicksell-Keynes-Hayek "connection," the source of trouble is to be found not in the market for goods or labor but rather in the market for financial assets.[6] The problem is that if our first-order conditions of intertemporal general equilibrium rule out from the start the existence of a rate of interest that would render saving and investment plans inconsistent, and thus in a state of disequilibrium, then we are likely to focus attention on the wrong "rigidity."[7]

When we begin with simultaneous intertemporal optimization, it is easy to see how we would end up here. Reflecting on his own role in translating Keynes into Walrasian form, Hicks would later remark, in reference to his construction of the "static" or atemporal elements of *Value and Capital*, that it had been a case of "taking step after step along a road which seemed pre-ordained as soon as one had taken the first step."[8] Though Hicks chose to shy away from general intertemporal equilibrium by opting instead for a temporary equilibrium approach, the Hicksian "week," he eventually conceded that "where I now feel that I went wrong was in my attempt to represent the markets of that week as being in equilibrium, even in 'general equilibrium,' in the sense of my static theory." That is, trying to collapse the effects of current transactions on expectations into the same time period "does deliberate violence to the *order* in which in the real world (in *any* real world) events occur," and "it was this device," he concluded, "this indefensible trick, which ruined the 'dynamic' theory of *Value and Capital*."[9] But unless we assume the economy to be in *actual* equilibrium at all times, equilibrium is impossible to define apart from dynamics; as Hicks put it, equilibrium "is a signal that time . . . has been put to one side."[10]

It is once we address the question of time and equilibrium in economics, however, that we must inevitably contend with capital. As Chris Bliss put it succinctly, "One of the essential tasks of a theory of capital is . . . to make clear why a purely static and timeless economic theory could not be adequate."[11] Recall that to Hayek's charge that Keynes had lifted Wicksellian natural-rate theory from its Böhm-Bawerkian foundations, Keynes replied: "Later on, I will endeavour to make good this deficiency."[12] According to Don Patinkin, he "of course did in *The General Theory*."[13] In Gerald O'Driscoll's words, "'Of course' Keynes did no such thing;" he was quite simply too nimble an economist to be overly encumbered by economic theory, or at least theory of metastasizing abstraction.[14] Where Keynes's a_i terms allowed for, but avoided elaborating, underlying machinations in relative prices, his assumption of unemployment rendered such concerns gratuitous. Indeed, as to how Keynes and Hayek, from a common Wicksellian heritage, should have nonetheless arrived at infamously opposed positions on matters of economic policy, we perhaps need look no further than this point.

Hayek, after all, was admittedly humbled by his protracted foray into the morass of capital theory, later remarking that once we permit more complex assumptions than the simple Böhm-Bawerkian parable, "Things become so damned complicated it's almost impossible to follow." He would go on to add that "like so many things, I am afraid, which I have attempted in economics, this capital theory work more shows a barrier to how far we can get in efficient explanations than sets forth precise predictions." The general complexity of the phenomena concerned and unknown character of the data "really much more point out limits to our possible knowledge than are contributions that make specific predictions possible."[15] It is, no doubt, a difficult task to discern any propitious scope for policy in an intricate system of time rates of return and continuous input functions.

Yet, it would be a mistake to therefore view our Wicksell connection as merely a sterile theoretical construct, internally consistent in the abstract but otherwise irrelevant to economics as practiced. The theoretical convergence that we have traced along Wicksellian lines was accompanied, though fundamentalist disciples of both economists would be loath to admit it, by noticeable convergence in the realm of policy as well. We have already seen evidence of Hayek's growing skepticism toward the capacity of relative prices to extricate an economy from a reverse cumulative process, once under way. In fact, his unease with what he had earlier dismissed as "secondary deflation" grew more acute in the wake of *Pure Theory of Capital*.[16] By 1975—at which point, we should note, "Keynesianism" of the vulgar, hubristic variety was already a spent force—Hayek would even go so far as to claim that "in the later stages of a depression when, in consequence of the appearance of extensive unemployment, the economy frequently is subjected to a cumulative process of contraction," he would be "the last to deny that, in these circumstances, monetary counteractions, deliberate attempts to maintain the money stream, are appropriate."[17] Hayek, moreover, also suggested that a dedicated policy of "employment through public works" may indeed be necessary to stem the cumulativeness of "secondary deflation."[18]

Nor was this convergence one-sided.[19] In his last article, published posthumously, Keynes pulled no punches in upbraiding some of his closest associates.[20] Waxing reflective, he criticized "modernist stuff, gone wrong and turned sour and silly," and sought instead to "remind contemporary economists that the classical teaching embodied some permanent truths of great significance."[21] For "in the long run," he insisted, "more fundamental forces may be at work, if all goes well, tending towards equilibrium... *natural* forces, one can call them."[22] He was certainly not talking about the other long-run equilibrium on which he has been more often quoted.[23] In fact, Hayek would later recount that on the last occasion he spoke with Keynes, he shared his concerns over the direction in which various of Keynes's disciples were extending his theories, to which Keynes cavalierly replied, "They are just fools. You know, my ideas were frightfully important in the 1930s. There was no question of combating inflation." According to Hayek, he then insisted, "But you can trust me, Hayek, my ideas have become dated. I'm going to turn public opinion around like this [snapping his fingers]."[24] Six weeks later, he was dead.

None of this should, in light of the Wicksell connection, come as a significant surprise. For it is the Wicksellian link that focuses both

Keynesian and Hayekian theory upon a unique economic problem; a problem *different* from that which ultimately detained the interest of the economics profession. That problem is how, even in a world *with* uncertainty and heterogeneous capital, a monetary economy is *nonetheless* capable of transcending the "dark forces of time and ignorance" to coordinate economic activity. As Keynes noted in his final article, pace Shackle and Robinson, "If it were not so, we could not have got on even so well as we have for many decades past."[25] In fact, Hayek was manifestly off the mark in his critique of Keynes's "economics of abundance," which, he claimed, ignored the crucial role of relative scarcity, even in the context of pervasive unemployment, in guiding production.[26] For Keynes himself conceded that "in general, the demand for some services and commodities will reach a level beyond which their supply is, for the time being, perfectly inelastic," such that even "whilst in other directions there is still a substantial surplus of resources," it will yet be the case that "as output increases, a series of 'bottle-necks' will be successively reached, where the supply of particular commodities ceases to be elastic and their prices have to rise to whatever level is necessary to divert demand into other directions."[27] Bottlenecks, indeed, would place Keynes firmly in the territory of the Ricardo effect.

The Wicksell connection, therefore, could be said to occupy a critical middle ground, between the radical uncertainty, and theoretical nihilism, of Shackle and Robinson, and period-zero, Walrasian-style *tâtonnement*. For Keynes and Hayek, equilibrium requires consistency of plans, plans that, while they may not be coordinated by the mythical Walrasian auctioneer (or his invisible hand), nor by the rational-expectations-charged representative agent of modern micro-founded macro models, can nonetheless be nudged toward mutual compatibility by continual market interactions and the iterative revision of expectations. But, insofar as plans do not coincide, the essential, deviation-counteracting functions of money may very well become deviation-amplifying. Here, Leijonhufvud's metaphor of a "corridor" of stability is perhaps instructive. Within the corridor, stocks of liquid assets may be adequate to buffer agents against unanticipated fluctuations in income, such that Hayek's might be the better guide to the dynamics of adjustment to new economic data. But, given a shock of sufficient magnitude, liquidity constraints may well give scope to Keynes's multiplier, and thus to the dynamics of income-constrained processes.[28]

This sort of analysis, indeed, lies at the very heart of the Wicksell connection, and it has no place whatsoever in any model of Walrasian descent, in which money is and only can be an "inessential property," a gratuitous finance or transaction constraint. As Frank Hahn pointed out, there is quite simply nothing the general equilibrium theorist can say about equilibrium in a monetary economy that he cannot say about the same economy under perfect barter, except perhaps that the former is less efficient than the latter (an inescapable conclusion that, of course, begs the question as to why money, credit, and banking even exist in the real world at all). What is more, where the Walrasian auctioneer or hyperrational representative agent effectively reconciles all plans before markets even open, it is difficult to explain how or why change should ever take place, when theoretically not only is change uncalled for, it in fact constitutes a contradiction of the entire Walrasian framework.

But for Hayek, as for Keynes, money, by its very nature, constitutes "a kind of loose joint" in the apparatus of the price system, bound at times to amplify errors in forecasts or expectations.[29] Change is thus an essential property of the system, and all *real* changes must work through *monetary* channels. Where those changes involve decisions across time, with all the attendant complications of uncertainty, the role of money is "bound to lead to constant fluctuations of economic activity," the more so the greater the play in the joint.[30] The crucial question is hence to what reliable extent do these monetary influences, which may for some time distort the price structure as determined by real variables quite radically, in the process galvanize forces that will ultimately be re-equilibrating? In any case, it is clear that these influences will impinge, first and foremost, upon the aberrant price, namely, the rate of interest.

To be sure, the Wicksellian task that Hayek assigned himself, and Keynes agilely flanked, is a daunting one. It is nothing less than to integrate money and heterogeneous capital into a dynamic equilibrium theory of the business cycle. As we have seen, such a task demands that we somehow resolve the tension between physical and financial, or value conceptions of capital, and also confront the notion of equilibrium not as a static outcome but as a process in time. Describing the importance of dynamics in economic analysis, we again quote Hayek:

> When it is used in contrast to equilibrium analysis in general, it refers to an explanation of the economic process as it proceeds in time, an explanation in terms of causation which must necessarily be treated as a chain of historical sequences. What we find here is not mutual interdependence between all phenomena but a unilateral dependence of the succeeding event on the preceding one. This kind of causal explanation of the process in time is of course the ultimate goal of all economic analysis, and equilibrium analysis is significant only in so far as it is preparatory to this main task.[31]

To anyone familiar with the so-called Cambridge capital controversies of the 1960s, this will strike an eerily familiar chord. Consider Joan Robinson:

> It is an absurd, though unfortunately common, error to suppose that substitution between labour and capital is exhibited by a movement from one point to another along a pseudo-production

> function. Each point represents a situation in which prices and wages have been expected, over a long past, to be what they are today, so that all investments have been made in the form that promises to yield the maximum net return to the investor. The effect of a change in factor prices cannot be discussed in these terms. Time, so to say, runs at right angles to the page at each point on the curve. To move from one point to another we would have either to rewrite past history or embark upon a long future.[32]

Hayek and Robinson both, as it were, get to the heart of what the Cambridge Capital Controversies were all about; having failed to provide a one-directional, causal explanation of capital intensity, Neoclassical economics essentially retreated to a defense of simultaneous equations and general equilibrium.[33] After all, if ambiguous causality and time are causing problems, then why not withdraw to an atemporal model of interdependent variables? The Cambridge Keynesians might thus have been better served had they recognized their common cause with Hayek in 1941, rather than belatedly joining a battle over the tedium of measuring capital that Hayek had long since deemed a sideshow.

We began by considering the parameters of the Keynesian "revolution." Whatever that revolution was, it was short-lived, quickly subsumed under the hegemony of general equilibrium theorizing. While it is beyond the scope of this study to investigate the reasons for the imperial ascendance of the Walrasian over the Wicksellian method in macroeconomics, it is worth emphasizing how fundamentally corrosive the capital-theoretic complications of Wicksell's model were to his general approach. Ultimately, it was far easier for economists to collapse the problem of capital and time into simple, one-commodity models with malleable, or "putty," capital, or else to resort to the metastatic world of Walrasian general equilibrium. For this reason, understanding the Keynesian *and*

Hayekian variations, and advances, on the Wicksellian theme may offer a way forward.

But, more than that, the polemics surrounding the "Keynes versus Hayek" debate have tended to obfuscate the very issues at which both economists were driving. For both economists, as for Wicksell before them, the concept of equilibrium was useful not as a description of any actual terminal state, but rather as an analytical stepping stone toward explaining economic dynamics *outside* of equilibrium, given that in any real-world historical process, disequilibrium, particularly of the intertemporal variety, is the rule rather than the exception. Constructing a theoretical account of changes in output and inflation upon the foundation of intertemporal optimization in continuous equilibrium is, therefore, to sever the Wicksell connection. Hicks was, in this respect, mistaken; the question ought not to be "which was right, Keynes *or* Hayek," but rather what can we learn from Keynes *and* Hayek?

NOTES

1. Olivier Blanchard, "The State of Macro," NBER Working Paper No. 14259 (August 2008), 26.
2. Ibid., 8, 24.
3. V. V. Chari, Patrick J. Kehoe, and Ellen R. McGrattan, "New Keynesian Models: Not Yet Useful for Policy Analysis," *American Economic Journal: Macroeconomics* 1 (2009): 242–266.
4. Michael Woodford, "Convergence in Macroeconomics: Elements of the New Synthesis," *American Economic Journal: Macroeconomics* 1 (2009): 267–279.
5. Note that since the New Keynesian construction ignores investment, we can no longer use our earlier loanable funds graphical framework.
6. For an excellent analysis of New Keynesian, or "neo-Wicksellian," dynamic stochastic general equilibrium modeling and its relation to Wicksell and Keynes, see Mauro Boianovsky and Hans-Michael Trautwein, "The New Neoclassical Synthesis and the Wicksell-Keynes Connection," in *The Return to Keynes*, ed. Bradley Bateman, Toshiaki Hirai, and Maria Cristina Marcuzzo (Cambridge, MA: Harvard University Press, 2010), 108–127. Also, Hiroshi Yoshikawa, "The *General Theory*: Toward the Concept of Stochastic Macro-Equilbrium," in *The*

Return to Keynes, ed. Bradley Bateman, Toshiaki Hirai, and Maria Cristina Marcuzzo (Cambridge, MA: Harvard University Press, 2010), 148–165.
7. Ibid., 124.
8. J. R. Hicks, *Economic Perspectives: Further Essays on Money and Growth* (Oxford: Oxford University Press, 1977), preface.
9. Ibid. See also Axel Leijonhufvud, "The Metamorpheses of Neoclassical Economics," in *Evolution of the Market Process: Austrian and Swedish Economics*, ed. Michel Bellet, Sandye Gloria-Palermo, and Abdallah Zouache (New York: Routledge, 2005), 12–13.
10. J. R. Hicks, "Some Questions of Time in Economics," in *Evolution, Welfare and Time in Economics*, ed. A. M. Tang, F. M. Westfield, and J. S. Worley (Lexington, MA: Lexington Books, 1976), 140.
11. Christopher Bliss, *Capital Theory and the Distribution of Income* (Amsterdam: North-Holland, 1975), 346.
12. J. M. Keynes, "The Pure Theory of Money: A Reply to Dr. Hayek," *Economica* 11 (1931): 395.
13. Don Patinkin, "Keynes' Monetary Thought: A Study of Its Development," *History of Political Economy* 8 (1976): 57.
14. Gerald P. O'Driscoll, *Economics as a Coordination Problem: The Contributions of Friedrich A. Hayek* (Kansas City, MO: Sheed Andrews and McMeel, 1977), 84.
15. F. A. Hayek, interview by Jack High, 1983, UCLA Oral History Program, in *Hayek on Hayek: An Autobiographical Dialogue*, ed. Stephen Kresge and Leif Wenar (London: Routledge, 1994), 141–142.
16. In a letter to Joan Robinson dated March 17, 1941, Hayek contended that while he was "not a strong advocate of lowering interest... in the early stages of the depression," on account of the fact that doing so would serve only to prop up an unsustainable investment structure, he nonetheless had "no objection against speeding up the downward movement [of the interest rate] in the later stages if that is needed." F. A. Hayek to J. V. Robinson, March 17, 1941, Papers of Joan Robinson, Kings College Archives, University of Cambridge, Cambridge.
17. F. A. Hayek, *A Conversation with Friedrich Hayek* (Washington, DC: American Enterprise Institute for Public Policy Research, 1975), 5. It is likely that Hayek withheld endorsement of more activist economic intervention throughout much of the 1950s and 1960s on account of the fact that his primary concern, during that period, was inflation. His reflections on Keynesian economics thus changed tone toward the end of the 1970s and into the 1980s. See Bruce Caldwell, "Why Didn't Hayek Review Keynes's *General Theory*?," *History of Political Economy* 30 (1998): 545–569.
18. F. A. Hayek, *New Studies in Philosophy, Politics, Economics and the History of Ideas* (London: Routledge and Kegan Paul, 1978), 212.

19. Hayek was in fact adamant (though certainly for potentially biased reasons) that Keynes was not a Keynesian in the mold of Robinson and Kahn. In particular, he noted Keynes's ardent opposition to inflation during the war and immediately after. F. A. Hayek, "Personal Recollections of Keynes and the 'Keynesian Revolution,'" *Oriental Economist* 34 (1966): 79; Nate White et al., "Symposium on Keynes: Why?," *Christian Science Monitor*, September 11, 1959, 13; F. A. Hayek, interview by W. W. Bartley III, 1984, in *Hayek on Hayek: An Autobiographical Dialogue*, ed. Stephen Kresge and Leif Wenar (London: Routledge, 1994), 91, 96–97.
20. The article had in fact been read by Keynes at the Political Economy Club on February 2, 1946. Economist Harry Johnson, present at the meeting, later wrote that Keynes exhibited "extreme rudeness" toward Joan Robinson and gave the impression that the paper "was aimed partly at her." Harry G. Johnson, "The Shadow of Keynes," in *The Shadow of Keynes: Understanding Keynes, Cambridge and Keynesian Economics*, ed. E. S. Johnson and H. G. Johnson (Oxford: Blackwell, 1978), 159.
21. J. M. Keynes, "The Balance of Payments of the United States," *Economic Journal* 56 (1946): 185–186.
22. Ibid.
23. That is, "In the long run we are all dead."
24. Hayek, *Hayek on Hayek*, 92. Hayek actually recounted this story on at least four separate occasions. See also F. A. Hayek, "The Keynes Centenary: The Austrian Critique," *Economist*, June 11, 1983, 45; Hayek, *New Studies in Philosophy, Politics, Economics*, 287; Hayek, "Personal Recollections," 79.
25. Keynes, "Balance of Payments," 185.
26. F. A. Hayek, *The Pure Theory of Capital* (1941; reprint, Chicago: University of Chicago Press, 1975), 373–377.
27. J. M. Keynes, *The General Theory of Employment, Interest and Money* (1936; reprint, London: Macmillan, 1981), 300–301.
28. See Elisabetta De Antoni, "The Auctioneerless Economics of Axel Leijonhufvud: the 'Dark Forces of Time and Ignorance' and the Coordination of Economics Activity," *Cambridge Journal of Economics* 30 (2006): 95. See also David Laidler, "The Monetary Economy and the Economic Crisis," Duke University Center for the History of Political Economy Working Paper No. 2011–04 (January 2011): 14–15.
29. Hayek, *Pure Theory*, 408. A *joint* in that it links the ability to demand with the willingness to supply, but a *loose* one in that it permits a nonvulgar interpretation of Say's law. See R. W. Garrison, "Time and Money: The Universals of Macroeconomic Theorizing," *Journal of Macroeconomics* 6 (1984): 197–213.
30. Hayek, *Pure Theory*, 407.

31. Hayek, *Pure Theory of Capital*, 17.
32. Joan Robinson, *Economic Heresies* (London: Basic Books, 1971), 103–104.
33. Avi J. Cohen and G. C. Harcourt, "Capital Theory Controversy: Scarcity, Production, Equilibrium and Time," in *Capital Theory*, Christopher Bliss, Avi J. Cohen, and G. C. Harcourt, vol. 1 (Cheltenham, UK: Elgar, 2005), xxxiv.

ACKNOWLEDGEMENTS

The intellectual debts owed for this work do, I fear, far exceed my ability to repay in thanks here. First and foremost, I must express my gratitude for the long-suffering support and supervision of Charles Maier, Emma Rothschild, and James Medoff, without whom this project could scarcely have been undertaken, let alone realized, and also to the keen (and often indispensably critical) counsel of Robert Solow and Andrew Gamble. To Geoff Harcourt, David Laidler, Niall Ferguson, and the late Paul Samuelson I owe considerable thanks for innumerable comments, criticisms, and suggestions, and hope that the finished product does not render too great a disservice to their contributions. Paul Davidson, Sheila Dow, Heinz Kurz, Steve Marglin, Martin Daunton, Avi Cohen, Angus Burgin, and Constantinos Repapis likewise offered comments and suggestions which no doubt attenuated the final error count, for which the author is alone responsible.

I must also extend thanks to Will Hamilton for astute research assistance and manuscript preparation—tasks to which he brought impeccable discernment and, no less importantly, superlative English wit. Conversations with Madsen Pirie, Alasdair

McLean-Foreman, and Lillian Lau consistently challenged me to think in new and more applicable ways.

I further salute the teams at Oxford University Press and Newgen, particularly Susan Ecklund, Catherine Rae, Terry Vaughn, Pete Mavrikis, Jaimee Biggins, Joe Jackson, and Molly Morrison, whose professionalism, thoroughness, efficiency, and, above all, good humor made them truly an honor and privilege to work with. It is unfortunate that it is precisely the excellence of their collaboration that conceals its size and extent. To Susan, especially, I tip my hat.

Thanks are owed also to workshop participants at the Harvard-Cambridge Joint Centre for History and Economics, to the Centre itself for generous financial and administrative support, and to the staff of the King's College and Trinity College Archives at the University of Cambridge. Permissions for quotation were kindly provided by Houghton Mifflin Harcourt Publishing Company, for J.M. Keynes, *The General Theory of Employment, Interest and Money* (1936; reprint, Harcourt, Brace and World, Inc., 1965); University of Chicago Press, for F.A. Hayek, "Three Elucidations of the Ricardo Effect." *Journal of Political Economy* 77 (1969): 274–285; and Oxford University Press, for Axel Leijonhufvud, *Information and Coordination: Essays in Macroeconomic Theory* (Oxford: Oxford University Press, 1981).

Finally, it must be noted that the longest-term debts have a tendency to compound over time to quite considerable sums. Mom, Dad, and Izzy—this work is as much yours as mine. Thank you.

BIBLIOGRAPHY

Archives

Haberler, Gottfried. Papers. Hoover Institution Archives. Stanford University, Stanford.
Kahn, Richard. Papers. Kings College Archives. University of Cambridge, Cambridge.
Kaldor, Nicholas. Papers. Kings College Archives. University of Cambridge, Cambridge.
Robinson, J. V. Papers. Kings College Archives. University of Cambridge, Cambridge
Sraffa, Piero. Papers. Trinity College Archives. University of Cambridge, Cambridge.

Other Sources

Alchian, A. "The Rate of Interest, Fisher's Rate of Return over Cost, and Keynes' Internal Rate of Return." *American Economic Review* 45 (1955): 938–943.
Arrow, K. J. "The Role of Price Adjustment." In *The Allocation of Economic Resources*, ed. M. Abramovitz. Stanford, CA: Stanford University Press, 1959.
Arrow, K. J., and G. Debreu. "Existence of an Equilibrium for a Competitive Economy." *Econometrica* 22 (1954): 265–290.
Asimakopulos, A. "The Determination of Investment in Keynes' Model." *Canadian Journal of Economics* 4 (1971): 382–388.

Ball, Laurence M. and David H. Romer. "Sticky Prices as Coordination Failure." *American Economic Review* 81 (1991), 539–52.

Barens, I., and V. Caspari. "Own-Rates of Interest and Their Relevance for the Existence of Underemployment Equilibrium Positions." In *A "Second Edition" of The General Theory*, ed. G. C. Harcourt and P. A. Riach. Vol. 1. London: Routledge, 1997.

Barro, R., and H. Grossman. "A General Disequilibrium Model of Income and Employment." *American Economic Review* 61 (1971): 82–93.

———. *Money, Employment and Inflation*. Cambridge: Cambridge University Press, 1976.

Bellet, Michel, Sandye Gloria-Palermo, and Abdallah Zouache, eds. *Evolution of the Market Process: Austrian and Swedish Economics*. New York: Routledge, 2005.

Benassy, J. P. "Neo-Keynesian Disequilibrium Theory in a Monetary Economy." *Review of Economic Studies* 42 (1975): 503–523.

Bernanke, Ben. "Nonmonetary Effects of the Financial Crisis in the Propagation of the Great Depression." *American Economic Review* 73 (1983): 157–76.

Bernanke, Ben, and Mark Gertler. "Agency Costs, Net Worth, and Business Fluctuations." *American Economic Review* 79 (1989): 14–31.

Blanchard, Olivier. "The State of Macro." NBER Working Paper No. 14259 (August 2008).

Blaug, Mark. *Economic Theory in Retrospect*. 5th ed. Cambridge: Cambridge University Press, 1997.

Bliss, Christopher. *Capital Theory and the Distribution of Income*. Amsterdam: North-Holland, 1975.

———. "Equal Rates of Profit." In *The New Palgrave: A Dictionary of Economics*, ed. J. Eatwell, M. Milgate, and P. Newman. Vol. 2. London: Macmillan, 1987.

Boianovsky, Mauro and Hans-Michael Trautwein. "The New Neoclassical Synthesis and the Wicksell-Keynes Connection." In *The Return to Keynes*, ed. Bradley Bateman, Toshiaki Hirai, and Maria Marcuzzo. Cambridge, MA: Harvard University Press, 2010.

Boulding, K.E. "The Theory of a Single Investment." *Quarterly Journal of Economics* 49 (1935): 478.

Bruno, M., E. Burmeister, and E. Sheshinski. "Nature and Implications of the Reswitching of Techniques." *Quarterly Journal of Economics* 80 (1966): 526–553.

Burmeister, Edwin. "Synthesizing the Neo-Austrian and Alternative Approaches to Capital Theory: A Survey." *Journal of Economic Literature* 12, no. 2 (1974): 413–456.

Caldwell, Bruce. "Why Didn't Hayek Review Keynes's *General Theory*?," *History of Political Economy* 30 (1998): 545–569.

Calvo, G. A. "Staggered Prices in a Utility Maximizing Framework." *Journal of Monetary Economics* 12 (1983): 383–398.

Caskey, J. and S. Fazzari. "Aggregate Demand Contractions with Nominal Debt Commitments: Is Wage Flexibility Stabilizing?" *Economic Inquiry* 25 (1987): 583–597.

Cass, David. "Optimum Growth in an Aggregative Model of Capital Accumulation." *Review of Economic Studies* 32 (1965): 233–240.

Chari, V.V., P. Kehoe, and E. McGrattan. "New Keynesian Models: Not Yet Useful for Policy Analysis." *American Economic Journal: Macroeconomics* 1 (2009): 242–66.

Christiano, Lawrence J., Martin Eichenbaum, and Charles L. Evans. "Nominal Rigidities and the Dynamic Effects of a Shock to Monetary Policy." *Journal of Political Economy* 113 (2005), 1–45.

Clark, P. *The Keynesian Revolution in the Making, 1924–1936*. Oxford: Clarendon Press, 1988.

Clower, Robert. "The Keynesian Counterrevolution: A Theoretical Appraisal." In *The Theory of Interest Rates*, ed. F. H. Hahn and F. P. R. Brechling. London: Macmillan, 1965.

Colander, David, Peter Howitt, Alan Kirman, Axel Leijonhufvud, and Perry Mehrling. "Beyond DSGE Models: Towards an Empirically-Based Macroeconomics." *American Economic Review, Papers and Proceedings* 98 (2008): 236–240.

Cohen, Avi. "Frank Knight's Position on Capital and Interest: Foundation of the Hayek/Knight/Kaldor Debate." In *The Economic Mind in America: Essays in the History of American Economics*, ed. M. Rutherford. London: Routledge, 1998.

———. "The Hayek/Knight Capital Controversy: The Irrelevance of Roundaboutness, or Purging Processes in Time?" *History of Political Economy* 35 (2003): 469–490.

Cohen, Avi and G. C. Harcourt. "Retrospectives: Whatever Happened to the Cambridge Capital Theory Controversies?" *Journal of Economic Perspectives* 17 (2003): 199–214.

———. "Introduction: Capital Theory Controversy: Scarcity, Production, Equilibrium and Time." In *Capital Theory*, ed. Christopher Bliss, Avi J. Cohen, and G. C. Harcourt. Vol. 1. Cheltenham: Edward Elgar, 2005.

Conard, J.W. *An Introduction to the Theory of Interest*. Berkeley: University of California Press, 1959.

Cottrell, A., and M. S. Lawlor. "'Natural Rate' Mutations: Keynes, Leijonhuvfud and the Wicksell Connection." *History of Political Economy* 23 (1991): 625–643.

Cowen, T. and R. Kroszner. "Money's Marketability Premium and the Microfoundations of Keynes's Theory of Money and Interest." *Cambridge Journal of Economics* 18 (1994): 379–390.

Davidson, D. "Om stabiliseringen af penningens värde" ("Concerning Stabilization of the Value of Money"). *Ekonomisk Tidskrift* 11 (1909): 1–25.

———. "Penningränta och varupris: Replik (till Wicksell)" ("The Money Rate of Interest and Commodity Prices: Reply [to Wicksell]"). *Ekonomisk Tidskrift* 11 (1909): 67–68.

Davidson, P. "Reviving Keynes' Revolution." *Journal of Post Keynesian Economics* 8 (1984): 561–575.

———. *Money and the Real World*. New York: Halstead, 1972.

———. *John Maynard Keynes*. London: Palgrave Macmillan, 2009.

De Antoni, Elisabetta. "The Auctioneerless Economics of Axel Leijonhufvud: The 'Dark Forces of Time and Ignorance' and the Coordination of Economic Activity." *Cambridge Journal of Economics* 30 (2006): 85–103.

DeLong, J. B. and L. H. Summers. "Is Increasing Price Flexibility Stabilizing?" *Journal of Money, Credit and Banking* 21 (1986): 481–497.

Desai, M. "The Task of Monetary Theory: The Hayek-Sraffa Debate in a Modern Perspective." In *Advances in Economic Theory*, ed. M. Baranzini. Oxford: Blackwell, 1982.

Diamond, Peter A. "National Debt in a Neoclassical Growth Model." *American Economic Review* 55 (1965): 1126–1150.

Eatwell, J., and M. Milgate, eds. *Keynes's Economics and the Theory of Value and Distribution*. London: Duckworth, 1983.

Ferguson, C.E. "The Specialization Gap: Barton, Ricardo, and Hollander." *History of Political Economy* 5 (1973): 1–13.

Ferguson, C .E., and Robert F. Allen. "Factor Prices, Commodity Prices, and the Switches of Technique." *Western Economic Journal* 8 (1970): 95–109.

Fisher, Irving. *The Rate of Interest*. New York: Macmillan, 1907.

———. "The Debt-Deflation Theory of Great Depressions." *Econometrica* 1 (1933): 337–357.

Galí, Jordí and Mark Gertler. "Inflation Dynamics: A Structural Econometric Analysis." *Journal of Monetary Economics* 44 (1999): 195-222.

Galí, Jordí, Mark Gertler, and David Lopez-Salido. "Robustness of Estimates of the Hybrid New Keynesian Phillips Curve." *Journal of Monetary Economics* 52 (2005), 1107-18.

Garegnani, P. "Notes on Consumption, Investment and Effective Demand." *Cambridge Journal of Economics* 2 (1978): 335–353.

———. "Notes on Consumption, Investment and Effective Demand." *Cambridge Journal of Economics* 3 (1979): 63–82.

Garretsen, H. *Keynes, Coordination and Beyond: The Development of Macroeconomics and Monetary Theory since 1945*. Aldershot: Edward Elgar, 1992.

Garrison, Roger. "Time and Money: The Universals of Macroeconomic Theorizing," *Journal of Macroeconomics* 6 (1984): 197–213.

———. *Time and Money: The Macroeconomics of Capital Structure*. London: Routledge, 2001.

Gordon, Robert. "Is Modern Macro or 1978-era Macro More Relevant to the Understanding of the Current Economic Crisis?" Paper presented at the International Colloquium on the History of Economic Thought, Sao Paulo, Brazil, August 3, 2009.

Haberler, Gottfried. *Prosperity and Depression*. 3d ed. Lake Success, NY: United Nations, 1946.

———. "Reflections on Hayek's Business Cycle Theory." *Wirtschafts Politische Blätter* 36 (1989): 220–230.

Hagemann, Harald, and Heinz D. Kurtz. "The Return of the Same Truncation Period and Reswitching in Neo-Austrian and More General Models." *Kyklos* 29 (1976): 678–708.

Hahn, Frank H. "On the Foundations of Monetary Theory." In *Essays in Modern Economics*, ed. M. Parkin. London: Longman, 1973.

———. "General Equilibrium Theory." In *The Crisis in Economic Theory*, ed. D. Bell and I. Kristol. New York: Basic Books, 1981.

———. *Money and Inflation*. Oxford: Blackwell, 1982.

———. "The Neo-Ricardians." *Cambridge Journal of Economics* 6 (1982): 353–374.

Hansen, Alvin. *A Guide to Keynes*. New York: McGraw-Hill, 1953.

Harcourt, G. C. "Some Cambridge Controversies in the Theory of Capital." *Journal of Economic Literature* 7 (1969): 369–405.

———. *Some Cambridge Controversies in the Theory of Capital*. Cambridge: Cambridge University Press, 1972.

Harrod, R. F. "Keynes the Economist." In *The New Economics*, ed. S. E. Harris. New York: Knopf, 1947.

———. *The Life of John Maynard Keynes*. London: Macmillan, 1951.

Hawtrey, Ralph. *Capital and Employment*. 2d ed. London: Longmans, Green & Co., 1952.

Hayek, F. A. "The 'Paradox' of Saving." *Economica* 32 (1931): 125–169.

———. *Prices and Production*. 2d ed. 1931. Reprint, London: Routledge and Kegan Paul, 1935.

———. "Reflections on the Pure Theory of Money of Mr. J. M. Keynes." *Economica* 11 33 (1931): 270–295.

———. "A Rejoinder to Mr. Keynes." *Economica* 11 (1931): 398–403.

———. "Money and Capital: A Reply to Mr. Sraffa." *Economic Journal* 42 (1932): 237–249.

———. "Reflections on the Pure Theory of Mr. J. M. Keynes (Continued)." *Economica* 12 (1932): 22–44.

———. *Monetary Theory and the Trade Cycle*. London: Jonathan Cape, 1933.

———. "Capital and Industrial Fluctuations." *Econometrica* 2 (1934): 152–167.

———. "On the Relationship between Investment and Output." *Economic Journal* 44 (1934): 207–231.
———. "The Mythology of Capital." *Quarterly Journal of Economics* 50 (1936): 199–228.
———. "Economics and Knowledge." *Economica* 4 (1937): 33–54.
———. "Investment That Raises the Demand for Capital." *Review of Economic Statistics* 19 (1937): 174–177.
———. "Profits, Interest and Investment." In *Profits, Interest and Investment and Other Essays on the Theory of Industrial Fluctuations.* London: Routledge, 1939.
———. *Pure Theory of Capital.* 1941. Reprint, Chicago: University of Chicago Press, 1975.
———. "[Professor Hayek and the Concertina-Effect]: A Comment." *Economica* 9 (1942): 383–385.
———. "The Ricardo Effect." *Economica* 9 (1942): 127–152.
———. "The Use of Knowledge in Society." *American Economic Review* 35 (1945): 519–530.
———. "Personal Recollections of Keynes and the 'Keynesian Revolution.'" *Oriental Economist* 34 (1966): 78–80.
———. "Three Elucidations of the Ricardo Effect." *Journal of Political Economy* 77 (1969): 274–285.
———. *New Studies in Philosophy, Politics, Economics and the History of Ideas.* London: Routledge and Kegan Paul, 1978.
———. "The Keynes Centenary: The Austrian Critique." *Economist,* June 11, 1983, 45–48.
———. *Hayek on Hayek: An Autobiographical Dialogue,* ed. Stephen Kresge and Leif Wenar. London: Routledge, 1994.
Hirshleifer, J. "On the Theory of the Optimal Investment Decision." *Journal of Political Economy* 66 (1958): 329–352.
Hicks, J. R. "Mr. Keynes and the 'Classics': A Suggested Interpretation." *Econometrica* 5 (1937): 147–159.
———. *Value and Capital.* Oxford: Clarendon Press, 1939.
———. "The Hayek Story." In *Critical Essays in Monetary Theory.* Oxford: Oxford University Press, 1967.
———. "The Austrian Theory of Capital and Its Rebirth in Modern Economics." In *Carl Menger and the Austrian School of Economics,* ed. J. R. Hicks and W. Weber. Oxford: Clarendon Press, 1973.
———. *Capital and Time: A Neo-Austrian Theory.* Oxford: Clarendon Press, 1973.
———. "Some Questions of Time in Economics." In *Evolution, Welfare and Time in Economics,* ed. A. M. Tang, F. M. Westfield, and J. S. Worley. Lexington, MA: Lexington Books, 1976.
———. *Economic Perspectives: Further Essays on Money and Growth.* Oxford: Oxford University Press, 1977.

Howitt, Peter. "Keynes's Theory of Own-Rates of Interest." In *Essays on Economic Stability and Growth*, ed. N. Kaldor. London: Duckworth, 1960.

———. "Coordination Failures." In *An Encyclopedia of Macroeconomics*, ed. Brian Snowdon and Howard R. Vane. Cheltenham, UK: Edward Elgar, 2003.

———. "The Microfoundations of the Keynesian Multiplier Process." *Journal of Economic Interaction and Coordination* 1 (2006): 33–44.

Howson, Susan. "Why Didn't Hayek Review Keynes's *General Theory*? A Partial Answer." *History of Political Economy* 33 (2001): 369–374.

Jenn-Treyer, Olivier. "The 'Wicksell Connection' and the Austrian Theory of Capital: Which Connections?" In *Evolution of the Market Process: Austrian and Swedish Economics*, ed. Michel Bellet, Sandye Gloria-Palermo and Abdallah Zouache. London: Routledge, 2005.

Johnson, H. G. "The Shadow of Keynes." In *The Shadow of Keynes: Understanding Keynes, Cambridge and Keynesian Economics*, ed. E. S. Johnson and H. G. Johnson. Oxford: Blackwell, 1978.

Kahn, R. *The Making of Keynes'* General Theory. Cambridge: Cambridge University Press, 1984.

Kaldor, Nicholas. "Capital Intensity and the Trade Cycle." *Economica* 6 (1939): 40–66.

———. "Professor Hayek and the Concertina-Effect." *Economica*, n.s., 9 (1942): 359–382.

Kalecki, M. "The Principle of Increasing Risk." *Economica* 4 (1937): 440–447.

Keynes, J. M. *A Treatise on Money*. Vol. 1, *The Pure Theory of Money*. 1930. Reprint, London: Macmillan, 1953.

———. "The Pure Theory of Money. A Reply to Dr. Hayek." *Economica* 11 (1931): 387–397.

———. *The General Theory of Employment, Interest and Money*. 1936. Reprint, New York: Harcourt, Brace and World, Inc., 1965.

———. "The Balance of Payments of the United States." *Economic Journal* 56 (1946): 185–186.

———. *The Collected Writings of John Maynard Keynes*, ed.Donald Moggridge. Vol. 13, *The General Theory and After, Part I: Preparation*. London: Macmillan, 1973.

———. *The Collected Writings of John Maynard Keynes*, ed.Donald Moggridge. Vol. 14, *The General Theory and After, Part II: Defence and Development*. London: Macmillan, 1973.

———. *The Collected Writings of John Maynard Keynes*, ed.Donald Moggridge. Vol. 24, *The General Theory and After: A Supplement*. London: Macmillan, 1979.

Knight, Frank. *Risk, Uncertainty and Profit*. Chicago: University of Chicago Press, 1921.

———. "Capital, Time, and the Interest Rate." *Economica* 1 (1934): 257–286.

Kocherlakota, N. "Money Is Memory." *Journal of Economic Theory* 81 (1998): 232–251.

Kohn, Meir. "A Loanable Funds Theory of Unemployment and Monetary Disequilibrium." *American Economic Review* 71 (1981): 859–879.

Koopmans, Tjalling C. "On the Concept of Optimal Economic Growth." Cowles Foundation Discussion Papers 163. Cowles Foundation for Research in Economics, Yale University (1963).

Kregel, J. A. "Money, Expectations and Relative Prices in Keynes' Monetary Equilibrium." *Economie Appliquée* 35 (1982): 449–465.

———. "Hamlet without the Prince: Cambridge Macroeconomics without Money." *American Economic Review* 75 (1985): 133–139.

———. "The Multiplier and Liquidity Preference: Two Sides of the Theory of Effective Demand." In *The Foundations of Keynesian Analysis*, ed. A. Barrère. London: Macmillan, 1988.

———. "The Theory of Value, Expectations and Chapter 17 of The General Theory." In *A "Second Edition" of* The General Theory, ed. G. C. Harcourt and P. A. Riach. Vol. 1. London: Routledge, 1997.

Kurz, H. D. "The Hayek-Keynes-Sraffa Controversy Reconsidered." In *Critical Essays on Piero Sraffa's Legacy in Economics*, ed. H. D. Kurz. Cambridge: Cambridge University Press, 2000.

———. "Keynes, Sraffa, and the Latter's 'Secret Skepticism.'" In *The Return to Keynes*, ed. Bradley W. Bateman, Toshiaki Hirai, and Maria Cristina Marcuzzo. Cambridge, MA: Harvard University Press, 2010.

Kydland, F. E., and E. C. Prescott. "Time to Build and Aggregate Fluctuations." *Econometrica* 50 (1982): 1345–1370.

Lachmann, Ludwig. "On Crisis and Adjustment." *Review of Economic Statistics* 21(1939): 62–68.

———. *Capital and Its Structure*. Kansas City, MO: Sheed Andrews and McMeel, 1956.

———. *Capital, Expectations, and the Market Process: Essays on the Theory of the Market Economy*. Kansas City, MO: Sheed Andrews and McMeel, 1977.

———. "Austrian Economics under Fire: The Hayek-Sraffa Duel in Retrospect." In *Austrian Economics: Historical and Philosophical Background*, ed. W. Grassl and B. Smith. New York: New York University Press, 1986.

———. *Expectations and the Meaning of Institutions: Essays in Economics*. London: Routledge, 1994.

Laidler, David. "Taking Money Seriously." *Canadian Journal of Economics* 21 (1988): 687–713.

———. *Fabricating the Keynesian Revolution: Studies in the Interwar Literature on Money, the Cycle, and Unemployment*. Cambridge: Cambridge University Press, 1999.

———. "Woodford and Wicksell on 'Interest and Prices': The Place of the Pure Credit Economy in the Theory of Monetary Policy." *Journal of the History of Economic Thought* 28 (2006): 151–159.

———. "Lucas, Keynes and the Crisis." *Journal of the History of Economic Thought* 32 (2010): 39–62.

———. "The Monetary Economy and the Economic Crisis." Duke University Center for the History of Political Economy Working Paper No. 2011–04 (January 2011).

Lawlor, M. S. *The Economics of Keynes in Historical Context: An Intellectual History of the* General Theory. New York: Palgrave, 2006.

Lawlor, M.S. and B. Horn. "Notes on the Sraffa-Hayek Exchange." *Review of Political Economy* 4 (1992): 317–340.

Lawson, T. "Uncertainty and Economic Analysis." *Economic Journal* 95 (1985): 909–927.

Leijonhufvud, Axel. *On Keynesian Economics and the Economics of Keynes: A Study in Monetary Theory*. London: Oxford University Press, 1968.

———. "The Wicksell Connection: Variations on a Theme." In *Information and Coordination: Essays in Macroeconomic Theory*. Oxford: Oxford University Press, 1981.

———. "Mr. Keynes and the Moderns." *European Journal of the History of Economic Thought* 5 (1998): 169–188.

———. "The Metamorphoses of Neoclassical Economics." In *Evolution of the Market Process: Austrian and Swedish Economics*, ed. Michel Bellet, Sandye Gloria-Palermo, and Abdallah Zouache. New York: Routledge, 2005.

Lerner, A. P. "The Essential Properties of Interest and Money." *Quarterly Journal of Economics* 66 (1952): 172–193.

———. "On the Marginal Product of Capital and the Marginal Efficiency of Investment." *Journal of Political Economy* 61 (1953): 1–14.

———. "Own-Rates and the Liquidity Trap." *Economic Journal* 72 (1962): 449–452.

Lindahl, E. R. "The Rate of Interest and the Price Level." In *Studies in the Theory of Money and Capital*. London: Allen and Unwin, 1939.

Lucas, R. E., Jr. "Expectation and the Neutrality of Money." *Journal of Political Economy* 4 (1972): 103–124.

———. "An Equilibrium Model of Business Cycles." *Journal of Political Economy* 83 (1975): 1113–1144

Lundberg, Erik. *Studies in the Theory of Economic Expansion*. London: P.S. King & Son, 1937.

Maclachlan, F.C. *Keynes's General Theory of Interest: A Reconsideration*. London: Routledge, 1993.

Machlup, Fritz. "Forced or Induced Savings: An Exploration into its Synonyms and Homonyms." *Review of Economics and Statistics* 25 (1943): 26–39.

———. "Hayek's Contribution to Economics." *Swedish Journal of Economics* 76 (1974): 498–531.

Mankiw, Gregory. "Real Business Cycles: A New Keynesian Perspective." *Journal of Economic Perspectives* 3 (1989): 79–90.

———. "The Reincarnation of Keynesian Economics." *European Economic Review*. 36 (1992): 559–565.

Marglin, Stephen. "Keynes without Nominal Rigidities." Harvard Institute of Economic Research Discussion Paper Number 1907 (2000).

Meltzer, A. *Keynes's Monetary Theory: A Different Interpretation*. Cambridge: Cambridge University Press, 1988.

Milgate, Murray. "Keynes on the 'Classical' Theory of Interest." *Cambridge Journal of Economics* 1 (1977): 307–315.

———. "On the Origin of the Notion of 'Intertemporal Equilibrium.'" *Economica* 46 (1979): 1–10.

Malinvaud, Edmond. "Capital Accumulation and Efficient Allocation of Resources," *Econometrica* 21 (1953): 233–268.

———. *The Theory of Unemployment Reconsidered*. Oxford: Basil Blackwell, 1977.

Meade, J.E. *The Cabinet Office Diary: 1944–1946*. In *The Collected Papers of James Meade*, ed. Susan Howson and Donald Moggridge. Vol. 6. London: Unwin Hyman, 1990.

Minsky, H.P. *John Maynard Keynes*. New York: Columbia University Press, 1975.

Modigliani, F. "Liquidity Preference and the Theory of Interest and Money." *Econometrica* 12 (1944): 45–88.

Moggridge, D. E. *Maynard Keynes: An Economist's Biography*. London: Routledge, 1992.

Moss, Laurence S., and Karen I. Vaughn. "Hayek's Ricardo Effect: A Second Look." *History of Political Economy* 18 (1986): 545–565.

Myrdal, G. *Monetary Equilibrium*. 1931. Reprint, London: William Hodge, 1939.

O'Driscoll, Gerald. *Economics as a Coordination Problem*. Kansas City, MO: Sheed, Andrews and McMeel, 1977.

Ohlin, B. Introduction to *Interest and Prices: A Study of the Causes Regulating the Value of Money*, by Knut Wicksell. 1898. Translated by R. F. Kahn. London: Macmillan, 1936.

———. "Some Notes on the Stockholm Theory of Savings and Investment I." *Economic Journal* 47 (1937): 53–69.

———. "Some Notes on the Stockholm Theory of Savings and Investment II." *Economic Journal* 48 (1937):, 221–240.

Panico, C. "The Evolution of Keynes's Thought on the Rate of Interest." *Contributions to Political Economy* 6 (1987): 53–61.

Pasinetti, Luigi L. "Wicksell Effects and Reswitching of Technique in Capital Theory." *Scandinavian Journal of Economics* 80 (1978): 181–189.

———. "The Marginal Efficiency of Investment." In *A "Second Edition" of The General Theory*, ed. G. C. Harcourt and P. A. Riach. Vol. 1. London: Routledge, 1997.

Pasinetti, Luigi L., Franklin M. Fisher, Jesus Felipe, J. S. L. McCombie, and Robert L. Greenfield. "Cambridge Capital Controversies." *Journal of Economic Perspectives* 17 (2003): 227–232.

Patinkin, Don. "Price Flexibility and Full Employment." *American Economic Review* 38 (1948): 543–564.

———. "Wicksell's 'Cumulative Process.'" *Economic Journal* 62 (1952): 835–847.

———. *Money, Interest and Prices*. 2d ed. New York: Harper and Row, 1965.

———. *Keynes' Monetary Thought: A Study of Its Development*. Durham, NC: Duke University Press, 1976.

———. "On Different Interpretations of the *General Theory*." In *John Maynard Keynes: Critical Assessments*, ed. John Cunningham. Vol. 8. London: Routledge, 1994.

Pigou, A. C. *Industrial Fluctuations*. 2nd ed. London: Macmillan, 1929.

———. "Mr. J. M. Keynes' *General Theory of Employment, Interest and Money*." *Economica* 3 (1936).

———. "The Classical Stationary State." *Economic Journal* 53 (1943): 343–351.

Ramsey, F.P. "A Mathematical Theory of Saving." *Economic Journal* 38 (1928): 543–559.

Rima, Ingrid Hahne. *Development of Economic Analysis*. London: Routledge, 2001.

Robbins, Lionel. *A History of Economic Thought: The LSE Lectures*. Edited by Steven G. Medema and Warren J. Samuels. Princeton, NJ: Princeton University Press, 1998.

Robertson, D. H. *Banking Policy and the Price Level*. London: Staples Press, 1926.

———. *Essays in Monetary Theory*. London: P. S. King, 1940.

Robinson, Joan. *The Economics of Imperfect Competition*. 1933. Reprint, London: Macmillan, 1969.

———. *The Accumulation of Capital*. 1956. Reprint, London: Palgrave Macmillan, 1969.

———. "Own Rates of Interest." *Economic Journal* 71 (1961): 596–600.

———. *Economic Heresies*. London: Basic Books, 1971.

———. "History versus Equilibrium." *Indian Economic Journal* 21 (1974): 202–213.

———. *Contributions to Modern Economics*. Oxford: Blackwell, 1978.

Rogers, C. *Money, Interest and Capital*. Cambridge: Cambridge University Press, 1989.

Rosser, John Barkley, Jr. *From Catastrophe to Chaos: A General Theory of Economic Discontinuities*. 2d ed. Norwell, MA: Kluwer Academic, 2000.

Runde, J. "Keynesian Uncertainty and Liquidity Preference." *Cambridge Journal of Economics* 18 (1994): 129–144.

Samuelson, Paul. "The General Theory." In *The New Economics*, ed. S. E. Harris. New York: Knopf, 1947.

———. "The General Theory." In *Keynes's "General Theory": Reports of Three Decades*, ed. R. Lekachman. London: Macmillan, 1964.

———. "A Summing Up." *Quarterly Journal of Economics* 80 (1966): 568–583.

Screpanto, Ernesto, and Stefano Zamagni. *An Outline of the History of Economic Thought*. Translated by David Field. New York: Oxford University Press, 2005.

Shackle, G. L. S. Foreword to *Value, Capital and Rent*, by Knut Wicksell. 1893. Translated by S. H. Frowein. London: Allen and Unwin, 1965.

———. *The Years of High Theory*. Cambridge: Cambridge University Press, 1967.

———. *Epistemics and Economics*. Cambridge: Cambridge University Press, 1973.

Skidelsky, Robert. *John Maynard Keynes*. Vol. 2, *The Economist as Savior 1920–1937*. London: Macmillan, 1983.

Solow, Robert M. *Capital Theory and Rate of Return*. Amsterdam: North-Holland, 1963.

———. "Towards a Macroeconomics of the Medium Run." *Journal of Economic Perspectives* 14 (2000): 151–158.

Sraffa, Piero. "Dr. Hayek on Money and Capital." *Economic Journal* 42 (1932): 42–53.

———. "A Rejoinder." *Economic Journal* 42 (1932): 249–251.

———. *Production of Commodities by Means of Commodities: Prelude to a Critique of Economic Theory*. Cambridge: Cambridge University Press, 1960.

Steele, G. R. *Keynes and Hayek: The Money Economy*. London: Routledge, 2001.

———. *The Economics of Friedrich Hayek*. 2d ed. London: Palgrave Macmillan, 2007.

Tieben, Bert. "Misunderstandings and Other Coordination Failures in the Hayek-Keynes Controversy." In *Austrian Economics in Debate*, ed. Willem Keizer, Bert Tieben, and Rudy van Zijp. London: Routledge, 1997.

Tobin, J. "The Interest Elasticity of the Transactions Demand for Cash." *Review of Economic Studies* 23 (1956): 241–247.

———. "Keynesian Models of Recession and Depression." *American Economic Review, Papers and Proceedings* 65 (1975): 195–202.

Townshend, Hugh. "Liquidity Premium and the Theory of Value." *Economic Journal* 47 (1937): 197–205.

Trautwein, Hans-Michael. "Endogenous Money: Modern Difficulties with the Wicksellian Approach." *Canadian Journal of Economics* 29 (1996): S229–S230.

Turvey, R. "Does the Rate of Interest Rule the Roost?" In *The Theory of the Rate of Interest*, ed. F. Hahn and F. P. R. Brechling. London: Macmillan, 1965.

von Neumann, J. "A Model of General Economic Equilibrium." *Review of Economic Studies* 13 (1945–1946): 1–9

Wicksell, Knut. *Value, Capital and Rent.* 1893. Translated by S. H. Frowein. London: Allen and Unwin, 1965.

———. *Interest and Prices: A Study of the Causes Regulating the Value of Money.* 1898. Translated by R. F. Kahn. London: Macmillan, 1936.

———. *Lectures on Political Economy.* Vol. 1, *General Theory.* Edited by Lionel Robbins. Translated by E. Classen. 1901. Reprint, London: Routledge and Kegan Paul, 1935.

———. *Lectures on Political Economy.* Vol. 2, *Money.* Edited by Lionel Robbins. Translated by E. Classen. 1906. Reprint, London: Routledge and Kegan Paul, 1935.

———. "Penningränta och varupris" ("The Money Rate of Interest and Commodity Prices"). *Ekonomisk Tidskrift* 11 (1909): 61–66.

Wilson, T. "Capital Theory and the Trade Cycle." *Review of Economic Studies* 7 (1940): 169–179.

Woodford, M. *Interest and Prices: Foundations of a Theory of Monetary Policy.* Princeton, NJ: Princeton University Press, 2003.

———. "Convergence in Macroeconomics: Elements of the New Synthesis." *American Economic Journal: Macroeconomics* 1 (2009): 267–79.

Yoshikawa, Hiroshi. "The *General Theory*: Toward the Concept of Stochastic Macro-Equilibrium." In *The Return to Keynes,* ed. Bradley Bateman, Toshiaki Hirai, and Maria Marcuzzo. Cambridge, MA: Harvard University Press, 2010.

INDEX